CW01183183

Active Learning in Higher Education

This insightful new book explores perspectives on active learning as creative discovery, conceptualisations of active learning spaces and transitions from theoretical approaches to active learning practice. It draws on the experiences of academics, learning technologists and clinical practitioners, and invites the reader to think about our conceptualisations of active learning and to move beyond mere demonstrations of its effectiveness.

With contributions from academics and NHS practitioners, this publication will make a unique contribution to the literature that increasingly points to the value, impact and reach of active learning pedagogy. It importantly addresses the need for active learning, highlighting some of the many theoretical issues that active learning raises through three broad lenses:

- The idea of active learning as creative play
- The use of theoretical models in designing active learning
- The transition from active learning theory to practice

Aimed at anyone with an interest in active learning as a pedagogical approach, *Active Learning in Higher Education* provides a starting point for further discussion and development of pedagogical theory, becoming an essential read for educators, school leaders as well as researchers in the field of education.

Wendy A. Garnham is co-founder of the Active Learning Network, a Reader in Psychology and Director of Student Experience for the Central Foundation Years at University of Sussex.

Isobel R. Gowers is Academic Lead for Active Inclusive Learning at Anglia Ruskin University and involved in the Active Learning Network both locally and globally.

The Staff and Educational Development Association Focus Series

The SEDA Focus series is for everyone interested in teaching, learning and assessment in higher education. Books in the Series are scholarly and practical, written by educational developers and researchers on up-to-the minute topics, bringing together experience and practice in a theoretical context. The Series is for educational, academic, staff and faculty developers, subject academics developing their professional teaching interests, institutional managers and everyone working to improve the quality of student learning. SEDA (The Staff and Educational Development Association) is the long-established professional association for staff and educational developers in the UK, promoting innovation and good practice in higher education.

Series Editor: Rebecca Turner
Titles in the series:

Active Learning in Higher Education
Theoretical Considerations and Perspectives
Edited by Wendy A. Garnham and Isobel R. Gowers

For more information about this series, please visit: https://www.routledge.com/SEDA-Focus-Series/book-series/SEDAF

Active Learning in Higher Education
Theoretical Considerations and Perspectives

Edited by
Wendy A. Garnham and
Isobel R. Gowers

Routledge
Taylor & Francis Group
LONDON AND NEW YORK

First published 2023
by Routledge
4 Park Square, Milton Park, Abingdon, Oxon OX14 4RN

and by Routledge
605 Third Avenue, New York, NY 10158

Routledge is an imprint of the Taylor & Francis Group, an informa business

© 2023 selection and editorial matter, Wendy A. Garnham and Isobel R. Gowers; individual chapters, the contributors

The right of Wendy A. Garnham and Isobel R. Gowers to be identified as the authors of the editorial material, and of the authors for their individual chapters, has been asserted in accordance with sections 77 and 78 of the Copyright, Designs and Patents Act 1988.

All rights reserved. No part of this book may be reprinted or reproduced or utilised in any form or by any electronic, mechanical, or other means, now known or hereafter invented, including photocopying and recording, or in any information storage or retrieval system, without permission in writing from the publishers.

Trademark notice: Product or corporate names may be trademarks or registered trademarks, and are used only for identification and explanation without intent to infringe.

British Library Cataloguing-in-Publication Data
A catalogue record for this book is available from the British Library

ISBN: 9781032418469 (hbk)
ISBN: 9781032418483 (pbk)
ISBN: 9781003360032 (ebk)

DOI: 10.4324/9781003360032

Typeset in Times New Roman
by codeMantra

Contents

Lists of Figures — vii
List of Tables — ix
List of Contributors — xi

Introduction to "Active Learning in Higher Education" — 1
WENDY GARNHAM

1 The University of Active Learning, Play and Storytelling – A thought-experiment about a different kind of institution — 6
TAB BETTS

2 Play not tell: Agency and becoming in the playful university — 19
ROY HANNEY

3 Bricolage as a holistic model for active learning — 27
SARAH HONEYCHURCH

4 The role of active learning in transformative learning and teaching experiences — 34
CHRISTINA MAGKOUFOPOULOU

5 Active cognitive tasks – Synthesising frameworks for active learning online — 46
MARY JACOB

6 Prospects for coactive learning — 57
SAM ELKINGTON

7 **From theory to practice – Active learning in the flow of clinical work** 66
NICK LENEY AND HELEN WINTER

8 **A contemplation on four active learning tasks: What do pedagogic theories suggest about them?** 73
PAOLO OPRANDI

Conclusion 82
ISOBEL GOWERS

Index 87

Figures

4.1 Informative and transformative active learning are an extension of the notions of informative and transformative learning (Engeström, 2001)   40
5.1 Bloom's taxonomy, revised version (Anderson and Krathwohl, 2001)   50

Tables

5.1 Cross-mapping Three Active Learning Frameworks 53
5.2 Mapping ABC LD with Online Engagement 54
7.1 Examples of Active v Passive Learning 68

Contributors

Tab Betts Tab Betts has been working to develop vision and leadership in active, inclusive and digitally enabled learning in higher education for over fifteen years and has won seven awards for his pedagogic collaborations and innovations. He co-founded the Active Learning Network: a global community for revolutionising learning, with satellite groups in the UK, Ireland, Greece, Germany, Romania, India, Cambodia, Nigeria and China. He has spoken at the House of Commons, is fluent in Mandarin Chinese, has served as Director of Online Learning and Innovation for the Parliamentary Centre of Asia and has delivered training and consultancy to clients around the world.
Twitter: @TabbanBetts
LinkedIn: https://www.linkedin.com/in/tabbetts/

Professor Sam Elkington Sam is Professor of Learning and Teaching at Teesside University where he leads the University's learning and teaching enhancement portfolio. Sam is a PFHEA and National Teaching Fellow (NTF, 2021) and has worked in higher education for over 15 years and has extensive experience working across teaching, research and academic leadership and policy domains. Most recently, Sam worked for Advance HE (formerly the Higher Education Academy) where he was national lead for Assessment and Feedback and Flexible Learning in Higher Education. Sam's latest book (Irons and Elkington, 2021) showcases the latest thinking in Enhancing Student Learning through Formative Assessment and Feedback.

Dr Wendy Garnham Reader in Psychology and Director of Student Experience for the Central Foundation Years, University of Sussex, UK. W.a.garnham@sussex.ac.uk.

As co-founder of the Active Learning Network, Wendy has experience of teaching across the educational spectrum from reception to postgraduate level, including leading a further education psychology department to Grade 1 status and leading a sixth form before returning to higher education. Wendy has won several awards for innovative teaching including a National Teaching Fellowship in 2020 and was part of a CATE award winning team for Foundation Year teaching in 2019.

Dr Isobel Gowers Academic Lead: Active Inclusive Learning, Anglia Ruskin University
Isobel's academic career started as a post-doctoral researcher before becoming a lecturer, course leader and finally taking leadership roles within higher education. She is actively involved in the Active Learning Network, both locally and globally. Her specialist interests include taking a holistic approach to active learning, from starting university to assessment and also using technology to support active learning both in the classroom and online.

Dr Roy Hanney Roy Hanney is employed at Solent University as a Course Leader for their Media Production programme. With close to twenty years of higher education teaching experience, he specialises in story, documentary, drama and transmedia production. His research interests include project-based learning and live projects which has formed the basis for a recently submitted PhD at Portsmouth University. He is a co-founder of DVMISSION 48 Hour Film Challenge and also works collaboratively with other organisations within the Solent area to promote opportunities for engagement with media practice.

Dr Sarah Honeychurch Good Practice Adviser, University of Glasgow. Sarah.Honeychurch@glasgow.ac.uk
Sarah has been working in HE for 25 years, first as a tutor and lecturer in Philosophy, then as a learning technologist before moving into academic development in recent years. She has a PhD in Education on the topic of participatory learning which she completed while working full time during a pandemic. Her current research interests are in participatory models of learning; remix; lurkers and authentic learning, teaching and assessment. Sarah co-founded and co-facilitates the Active Learning Network University of Glasgow Satellite. She blogs at https://www.nomadwarmachine.co.uk

Mary Jacob Mary Jacob is Lecturer in Learning and Teaching, Learning and Teaching Enhancement Unit, Aberystwyth University,

Wales, UK. Since 2017, Mary has served as the Coordinator for the Postgraduate Certificate in Teaching in Higher Education. In addition, she designs and facilitates training in educational practice for general university teaching staff. She has a passion for active learning, having used it in her previous role as Lecturer in Chinese language and literature at the University of California, Davis. She posts Weekly Resource Roundups on the LTEU blog (https://wordpress.aber.ac.uk/e-learning/) to support university staff and colleagues across the HE sector. mhj@aber.ac.uk

Nick Leney Professional Learning Lead – Novo Learning Limited (www.learningafresh.com), nick.leney@learningafresh.com
First trained as a teacher, Nick spent many years leading professional development within the secondary education sector, including the UK's largest fully online school. In 2020 Nick formed Novo Learning, a consultancy offering innovative professional development solutions. A strong advocate of disruptive learning strategy, Nick seeks to address mismatches in contemporary professionals' learning needs and the available training. Project work within health, education, law enforcement, defence, and the third sector has supported cross-professional insights and perspectives. In 2021 the ACTAsia's Caring for Life project authored by Nick was selected by the United Nations for inclusion in their SDG good practices case set. Nick holds a master's degree in educational leadership and a fellowship at the Learning and Performance Institute (UK). An active participant in the UCL ed-tech accelerator programme, Nick subsequently led a Knowledge Transfer Partnership with the University of South Wales investigating scaled online learning through artificial intelligence.

Dr Christina Magkoufopoulou Christina is a Senior Fellow of Advance HE and has had an extensive career within the UK and EU higher education in roles involving Academic Development, Science Teaching and Scientific Research. In her current role, within Coventry University, Christina is involved in the delivery of the Postgraduate Certificate in Academic Practice in HE (PGCAPHE) and provides academic development support in areas such as Curriculum Design and Technology Enhanced Learning. Christina's scholarly interests focus on Active Learning, Communities of Practice and Assessment and Feedback.

Dr Paolo Oprandi Senior Learning Technologist, University of Sussex, UK. paolo@sussex.ac.uk

Paolo is a Doctor in Education with an academic background which at different times has spanned the sciences, humanities and social sciences. He has worked in the area of learning technologies for 20 years and is currently a Senior Learning Technologist in the Technology Enhanced Learning team at the University of Sussex. His research has focussed on curriculum development that welcomes diversity into the academic disciplines, using the appropriate teaching, learning and assessment technologies.

Dr Helen Winter Dr Helen Winter MBBS DPhil is a consultant medical oncologist, SWAG Cancer Alliance Clinical Director and honorary senior research fellow at the University of Bristol. Having completed a Postgraduate Certificate of Medical Education in 2005, Helen has remained committed to multi-professional learning as an innovative and agile health service driver to deliver excellence in cancer care.

A genuine lifelong learner, Helen joined Green Templeton College, University of Oxford mid-career to complete doctoral research on imaging and circulating cancer biomarkers in hepatic malignancies. In addition to writing around this specialism, Helen has published and presented on medical education and currently works as a Training Programme Director for Medical Oncology in the South West.

Helen advocates strongly for improved equity in health outcomes across the South West region and has delivered innovative solutions through the Cancer Alliance, most recently, a novel venture with the private sector to use AI technology to accelerate the identification and matching of patients to trials, with the dual aim of improving outcomes and creating breakthroughs in cancer research.

SWAG Cancer Alliance Clinical Director and Consultant Medical Oncologist, Bristol Cancer Institute, UK. Helen.Winter@uhbw.nhs.uk

Introduction to "Active Learning in Higher Education"
Wendy Garnham

Higher Education is in flux. Prior to the COVID pandemic, the academic literature proliferated with evidence of the effectiveness of active learning strategies (e.g. Prince, 2004; Sivan et al., 2000; Kilgo et al., 2015) in promoting achievement and understanding in students, even though the students themselves may often rate it as less favourable than traditional lecture-based dissemination methods (Deslauriers et al., 2019; Lobo, 2017). In disciplines as diverse as STEM (Weir et al., 2019) peace and conflict studies (Sjöstedt, 2015) and psychology (Cherney, 2008), active learning has been shown to have beneficial outcomes for achievement, promoting inclusivity and for social interaction.

As the COVID pandemic took hold, we, as practitioners, were forced to develop active learning for online teaching spaces and to re-consider pedagogical practices that we had previously established. Hao et al. (2021) had previously pointed to the ease with which active learning could be conducted in an active learning classroom but how would it fare in an online environment? Thankfully Hao and colleagues identified that it was the pedagogical approach that was critical rather than the learning environment.

More recently, a return to the traditional lecture theatre learning space has been advocated by the government with this seen as the optimal learning environment for Higher Education. Thankfully, even in large lecture spaces, active learning has been demonstrated to improve engagement and achievement (e.g. Cavanagh, 2011; Smith and Cardaciotto, 2011) but we are now facing a different issue. Whilst students are encouraged to return, to engage with face-to-face teaching, many are too anxious to do so, particularly as the COVID pandemic continues.

Against this backdrop, active learning has continued to gain prominence in terms of its ability to engage students, close achievement gaps and to tackle some of the anxiety that students may bring as

DOI: 10.4324/9781003360032-1

they return to the classroom or lecture hall. We know, for example, that active learning can help to alleviate anxiety (Adkins-Jablonsky et al., 2021; Harper and Daane, 1998; Okebukola, 1986), it can eliminate gender achievement gaps in some subjects (Lorenzo, Crouch and Mazur, 2006), can provide more equitable outcomes for underrepresented student groups (e.g. Theobald et al., 2020; Haak et al., 2011) and can be a useful mechanism for reducing stress associated with assessments (Yoder and Hochevar, 2005; Khan and Madden, 2018). Chiu and Cheng (2017) report that students feel more engaged with their learning when active learning methods are used, and Svinicki and McKeachie (2014) identify higher levels of motivation in students when engaged in active learning tasks.

The literature on active learning has proliferated in recent years with suggestions of innovative and effective tools to ensure that students learn in a way that maximises critical thinking, discussion and debate and ultimately promotes achievement. The sheer range of active learning strategies is exhaustive including everything from using walking seminars (Bälter et al., 2018) to problem-based collaborative games (Ting, Lam and Shroff, 2019) to writing the lyrics for a song to promote second language learning (Demirci and Yavaslar, 2018). As the number and variety of active learning strategies continue to grow, the consideration of theoretical approaches to active learning has lagged somewhat behind. Bernstein (2018) was himself advocating the need to move beyond simply asking whether active learning works to a deeper consideration of the theoretical underpinnings of this pedagogical approach.

This book aims to address this need by exploring some of the many theoretical issues that active learning raises. We approach this task using three broad angles: We begin with a thought experiment presented by Tab Betts. Can theoretical models of active learning provide a transformative philosophy for university learning? Roy Hanney conceptualises the "active learning university", exploring the role of play in this university and using active learning as a key to unlocking "functional fixedness" in generating novel ideas to problems, and Sarah Honeychurch uses a socio-cultural theory called Bricolage to examine how active assessment might be built into this conceptualisation.

We then move, in Part 2, to exploring new theoretical frameworks that might be used in an active learning university. Christina Magkoufopoulou takes us on a journey through theoretical models of active learning to develop a new framework of transformative active learning, and Mary Jacob introduces four established models of active learning which she then synthesises into an integrated framework for active learning and student engagement.

In Part 3, we attempt to bridge the gap between theory and practice. Sam Elkington discusses the inter-relationships between active learning strategies that take place in different learning "spaces". How do we conceptualise active learning for online and face-to-face environments? Helen Winter and Nick Leney describe the theoretical underpinnings of Action-Based Learning as a high-impact methodology for clinical contexts and demonstrate how this can lead to the creation of a culture of learning, sharing, collaborating and doing, and Paolo Oprandi directs our attention to the way in which active learning approaches promote sociocultural engagement. Using four active learning tasks, Paolo attempts to demonstrate how pedagogic theory of active learning can explain how student become more attached to and feel a greater degree of expertise towards their learning.

Whilst we provide only a snapshot of the theoretical debates in this area, the aim is to begin to realign the balance between the sharing of examples of active learning and the consideration of the theoretical underpinnings of such tasks. As active learning continues to gain prominence in Higher Education settings, and its value is increasingly recognised in developing the individual learner, it is hoped that the stories told within these covers will serve as a starting point rather than a point of simple dissemination for the role of active learning in our institutions.

References

Adkins-Jablonsky, S. J., Shaffer, J. F., Morris, J. J., England, B., & Raut, S. (2021). A tale of two institutions: Analyzing the impact of gamified student response systems on student anxiety in two different introductory biology courses. *CBE—Life Sciences Education*, *20*(2), ar19.

Bälter, O., Hedin, B., Tobiasson, H., & Toivanen, S. (2018). Walking outdoors during seminars improved perceived seminar quality and sense of well-being among participants. *International journal of Environmental Research and Public Health*, *15*(2), 303.

Bernstein, D. A. (2018). Does active learning work? A good question, but not the right one. *Scholarship of Teaching and Learning in Psychology*, *4*(4), 290.

Cavanagh, M. (2011). Students' experiences of active engagement through cooperative learning activities in lectures. *Active Learning in Higher Education*, *12*(1), 23–33.

Chiu, P. H. P., & Cheng, S. H. (2017). Effects of active learning classrooms on student learning: a two-year empirical investigation on student perceptions and academic performance. *Higher Education Research & Development*, *36*(2), 269–279.

Cherney, I. D. (2008). The effects of active learning on students' memories for course content. *Active Learning in Higher Education*, *9*(2), 152–171.

Demirci, C., & Yavaslar, E. (2018). Active learning: let's make them a song. *Cypriot Journal of Educational Sciences, 13*(3), 288–298.

Deslauriers, L., McCarty, L. S., Miller, K., Callaghan, K., & Kestin, G. (2019). Measuring actual learning versus feeling of learning in response to being actively engaged in the classroom. *Proceedings of the National Academy of Sciences, 116*(39), 19251–19257.

Haak, D. C., HilleRisLambers, J., Pitre, E., & Freeman, S. (2011). Increased structure and active learning reduce the achievement gap in introductory biology. *Science, 332*(6034), 1213–1216.

Hao, Q., Barnes, B., & Jing, M. (2021). Quantifying the effects of active learning environments: separating physical learning classrooms from pedagogical approaches. *Learning Environments Research, 24*(1), 109–122.

Harper, N. W., & Daane, C. J. (1998). Causes and reduction of math anxiety in preservice elementary teachers. *Action in Teacher Education, 19*(4), 29–38.

Khan, A., & Madden, J. (2018). Active learning: A new assessment model that boost confidence and learning while reducing test anxiety. *International Journal of Modern Education and Computer Science, 11*(12), 1.

Kilgo, C. A., Ezell Sheets, J. K., & Pascarella, E. T. (2015). The link between high-impact practices and student learning: Some longitudinal evidence. *Higher Education, 69*(4), 509–525.

Lobo, G. J. (2017). Active learning interventions and student perceptions. *Journal of Applied Research in Higher Education*, 465–473.

Lorenzo, M., Crouch, C. H., & Mazur, E. (2006). Reducing the gender gap in the physics classroom. *American Journal of Physics, 74*(2), 118–122.

Okebukola, P. A. (1986). Relationships among anxiety, belief system, and creativity. *The Journal of Social Psychology, 126*(6), 815–816.

Prince, M. (2004). Does active learning work? A review of the research. *Journal of Engineering Education, 93*(3), 223–231.

Sivan, A., Leung, R. W., Woon, C. C., & Kember, D. (2000). An implementation of active learning and its effect on the quality of student learning. *Innovations in Education and Training International, 37*(4), 381–389.

Sjöstedt, R. (2015). Assessing a broad teaching approach: The impact of combining active learning methods on student performance in undergraduate peace and conflict studies. *Journal of Political Science Education, 11*(2), 204–220.

Smith, C. V., & Cardaciotto, L. (2011). Is active learning like broccoli? Student perceptions of active learning in large lecture classes. *Journal of the Scholarship of Teaching and Learning, 11*(1), 53–61.

Svinicki, M. D., & McKeachie, W. J. (2014). Active learning: Group-based learning. *McKeachie's Teaching Tips. 14th ed. Wadsworth.* Lexington: DC Health, 191–202.

Theobald, E. J., Hill, M. J., Tran, E., Agrawal, S., Arroyo, E. N., Behling, S, Chambwe, N., Laboy Cintrón, D., Cooper, J. D., Dunster, G., Grummer, J. A., Hennessey, K., Hsiao, J., Iranon, N., Jones II, L., Jordt, H., Keller, M., Lacey, M. E., Littlefield, C. E., Lowe, A., Newman, S., Okolo,

V., Olroyd, S., Peecook, B. R., Pickett, S. B., Slager, D. L., Caviedes-Solis, I. W., Stanchak, K. E., Sundaravardan, V., Valdebenito, C., Williams, C. R., Zinsli, K., & Freeman, S. (2020). Active learning narrows achievement gaps for underrepresented students in undergraduate science, technology, engineering, and math. *Proceedings of the National Academy of Sciences*, *117*(12), 6476–6483.

Ting, F. S. T., Lam, W. H., & Shroff, R. H. (2019). Active learning via problem-based collaborative games in a large mathematics university course in Hong Kong. *Education Sciences*, *9*(3), 172.

Weir, L. K., Barker, M. K., McDonnell, L. M., Schimpf, N. G., Rodela, T. M., & Schulte, P. M. (2019). Small changes, big gains: A curriculum-wide study of teaching practices and student learning in undergraduate biology. *PLoS One*, *14*(8), e0220900.

Yoder, J. D., & Hochevar, C. M. (2005). Encouraging active learning can improve students' performance on examinations. *Teaching of Psychology*, *32*(2), 91–95.

1 The University of Active Learning, Play and Storytelling – A thought-experiment about a different kind of institution

Tab Betts

Introduction

Once upon a time, in a future hopefully not too far away, there was a university – but not a university like any you have seen before. Imagine an institution where, instead of lectures, seminars, workshops, labs and tutorials, you had collaborative storytelling, creative play time and learning jamming sessions. This chapter will try to paint a picture of this hypothetical institution.

Before we begin, I would like to ask a favour: Please forget everything you know about HE.

Great. Feels better, doesn't it? Of course, it is impossible to forget everything, but we can try and – as every child knows – disruption and destruction are often just as satisfying as creation (if not more so). Now that we have knocked down the tower of bricks, we can start to build it up again, without being hampered by former preconceptions or baggage.

Which bricks should we use first? What kind of tower do we want to build? One great way of imagining new structures is to ask different questions. This chapter will aim to ask and answer three questions:

- What would a university look like if it took active learning seriously?
- What would a university look like if it took play seriously?
- What would a university look like if it took storytelling seriously?

The reader is also invited to use these three questions to reimagine their own university. As you read, try to ask yourself 'What would my university look like if it took X seriously?' and write your own answers to these questions. You are also strongly encouraged to share your reflections with the author of this chapter and with others. The ideas

DOI: 10.4324/9781003360032-2

in this chapter are some thoughts based on the author's current perspective, but there are many other possibilities. Only by reimagining and sharing these visions of alternative futures can we hope to change the culture of our institutions.

Imagining things is fun, but it is important to link these thoughts to theory and research. In trying to answer these questions, the chapter will explore how theoretical models and academic research on playful learning, game-based learning and gamification, as well as models of storytelling, such as Joseph Campbell's concept of the hero's journey, Dan Harmon's story circle and Aristotle's *Poetics*, could provide a transformative philosophy for facilitating a culture of active learning (e.g. Farmer, 2019; Fischer, 2019; Busch, Conrad & Steinicke, 2013). These may include elements of how play and stories make and break rules for curriculum design, group work, goal setting, radical inclusivity, radical thinking and creativity.

We will plumb the depths of teachers' and learners' own character arcs. We will leave our comfort zone and venture into the territory of transforming a module or topic into an interactive experiential story. We will discuss the architecture of how to take learners on a hero's journey that allows them to return home having overcome adversity and brought back the treasure and experiences that they were seeking. Join us on this thought-experiment about the University of Active Learning, Play and Storytelling.

Why do we need a different kind of university? And why active learning, play and storytelling?

The protagonist of this particular story is the University of Active Learning, Play and Storytelling (hereafter known as 'the University'). There has long been a connection made between learning, play and stories (Williams, Cooney & Nelson, 1999). However, the mainstream culture of universities, which focuses on traditional teacher-centred pedagogies and power relationships, often frowns on active learning, play and stories, deeming them inappropriate for higher education.

As we move from a world in which knowledge is scarce and can only be accessed through libraries and experts, to one in which knowledge is openly available to almost anyone via the internet, we need to rethink the role of teaching in higher education (Brown, cited in Race, 2019). Despite the resistance to change, traditional teacher-centred pedagogies are outmoded, inequitable and not in line with current research evidence (e.g. Deslauriers, McCarty, Mille, Callaghan & Kestin, 2019). Learning in universities needs to be revolutionised based on what we know about how learning happens. Active learning, play and storytelling provide three fundamental pillars of how human consciousness constructs and retains new knowledge, skills, beliefs and habits. There is a wealth of academic research to support the importance of these three elements in learning (e.g. Bovill, 2020; Deslauriers et al., 2019; Fischer, 2019; Van Schalkwyk & D'Amato, 2015; Kordaki & Agelidou, 2010; Tang & Yuen, 2016).

The inspiration for this idea came from a simple pen and paper storytelling game called *The Ground Itself* (Pipkin, 2019) in which players co-create a story about an imaginary place based on randomised prompts and questions. Given the highly creative results it produced, it seemed like an interesting model to apply to rethinking higher education.

I have already explored this concept in a workshop in which I invited participants to imagine their own version of university and add it to my session slides (Betts, 2021).

You may think that imagining a hypothetical university is a waste of time, and these outlandish ideas could never be implemented. However, if you consider predictions around the metaverse and immersive technologies, then you may start to realise that it is entirely possible that, in the very near future, we will be able to recreate universities in any image we can imagine. Even without that, partially fuelled by the impact of Covid-19, many universities are beginning to consider redesigning campus learning spaces, moving towards more diverse ways of working and more flexible approaches to teaching and learning. So the question becomes, if given a blank canvas to build or rebuild any kind of university, what kind of university would we build?

What do we know about the solution?

Why is active learning important? The cornerstone theory which underpins active learning is the idea of social constructivism. Knowledge is constructed in the learner's own mind, but also as an interaction between members of a community to co-construct knowledge (See Bovill, 2020). This is in contrast to early educational practices which theorised that learning functioned according to a transmission model, and learners were 'vessels to be filled'. Perhaps as a consequence of confirmation bias and cultural inertia, most people's concept of learning still hinges on teacher-centred approaches, despite growing evidence that active learning approaches result in better learning outcomes (e.g. Deslauriers et al., 2019).

Why is play important? We know from watching animals and small children that play is the primary way in which living creatures learn. Think of lion cubs wrestling with one another or a child trying to build a tower out of wooden blocks. Observing these phenomena can teach us that learning is iterative and that failure is an essential part of the process of refining those iterations. The importance of play and games in education has been widely recognised (Sidhu, Carter & Curwood, 2021; Abbott, 2018; Daniau, 2016; Zhang & Shang, 2015; Busch, Conrad & Steinicke, 2013).

Why is storytelling important? Research into neuroscience and psychology has demonstrated that human cognition, memory and imagination relies heavily on organising experiences according to narrative structures and sequential visualisations (See Moulton, 2014). Since ancient Greek times, memory experts have been using mnemonic techniques, such as the method of loci or memory palace, to enhance their ability to recall knowledge or memorise speeches, and these are still used in modern vocabulary learning (Wang, 2021; Amiryousefi, 2015). Other benefits of incorporating storytelling in education, such as learner motivation, flow states and authentic contexts for learning, have also been explored by numerous authors (e.g. Busch, Conrad & Steinicke, 2013; Kordaki & Agelidou, 2010; Williams, Cooney & Nelson, 1999).

What would the University look like?

Most universities are not fit for the purpose of learning. Controversial, yes, but also true. Many educators hold that motivation and curiosity are two of the key components of learning (e.g. Malone & Lepper, 2021; Malone, 1981). Think of your average university campus and, in most cases, you will see that it is ostensibly designed to do anything but excite people. So what would a motivating and curiosity-inspiring campus look like? It would be more like a video game. It would be more colourful, visually stimulating and aesthetically pleasing. It would have more spaces that were designed for interactivity, customisation and creative sandboxes for experimentation. This would draw on the notion of aesthetic curiosity and intellectual curiosity described in Malone and Lepper's model of intrinsically motivating instruction (Malone & Lepper, 2021; Malone, 1981).

The architecture itself and the layout of the campus and its learning spaces would stimulate curiosity. Wouldn't it be more exciting to journey to your classes if the campus was laid out like a theme park, with different themed zones for each area of the campus? For example, the humanities zone could have a theme based around ancient cultures, with replica statues and *Indiana Jones*-style ancient ruins. Engineering and informatics could be based around a science fiction, cyberpunk or steampunk concept, with a decorative theme based around spaceships, robots or a *Bladerunner*-esque futuristic city theme.

The university buildings would be designed to entertain and inspire, as well as being functional. There would be areas to play (e.g. Lego rooms, soft play rooms, gaming labs, performance spaces) and spaces for experimentation (e.g. innovation labs, disciplinary data sandboxes, maker spaces, simulation hubs).

Aspects of research in the discipline could be incorporated into the environment as interactive museum exhibits, such as the kind found in science museums around the world, but these would be pitched at university level, so that they could be used to directly complement the learning experience both inside and outside class time. This would allow anyone on campus to interact with, and contribute to, core knowledge and research within the discipline.

How can we transform a module or topic into an interactive experiential story?

At the University, staff and students would take traditional active learning course design and add a layer of collaborative storytelling to it. This approach would take a foundation of constructive alignment to ensure that all assessment tasks, teaching and learning activities and content are directly aligned to the achievement of intended learning outcomes (Biggs & Tang, 2011). However, the learning community of staff and students would create narrative layers around this pedagogical core. These would involve stories which encourage learners to put themselves in the situation of a character who is facing problems or challenges similar to those that the students may face when trying to apply their disciplinary learning in the real world. As the module progresses, the character might face different scenarios related to the topics covered in the learning activities and content. These aspects of the story could be complemented by experiential learning tasks which help learners to enact and reflect upon authentic, real-world applications of their subject knowledge.

This use of storytelling in learning design is supported by work on how stories can render learning more motivating (Malone & Lepper, 2021; Malone, 1981). This is achieved by stimulating imagination and using story-world contexts to connect elements of learning. Adding a story world context to your course may not only increase motivation, but also provide a memory palace-esque environment which helps learners to retain knowledge by linking it to visualisations, authentic scenarios and memorable environments (e.g. Wang, 2021; Amiryousefi, 2015).

What would a collaborative storytelling session look like?

In a collaborative storytelling session, students would be given a practical scenario related to the topic (see scenario-based Learning, e.g. Hursen & Fasli, 2017). This would provide a sand-pit for exploration and problem-solving, in which learners exercise higher order thinking skills at the upper end of Bloom's Taxonomy, such as analysing, evaluating, synthesising and creating. Drawing on ideas from pen and paper roleplaying games (e.g. Abbott, 2018; Daniau, 2016; Lean, Illingworth & Wake, 2018; Sidhu & Carter, 2021; Sidhu, Carter & Curwood, 2021), one or two students within each group could act as storyteller-troublemakers. Their job would be to describe the evolving scenario, provide problems or challenges for the group to solve and describe how the scenario responds to decisions made by the group. More information on this approach can be found in my chapter on Story-Game Based Learning in the upcoming Active Learning Network publication (Betts, in press).

What would creative play time look like?

In creative play time, a learning community, consisting of students, tutors and possibly stakeholders from a variety of different backgrounds, comes together to play with challenging problems and concepts from their learning to experiment with possible solutions and exercise their creative thinking skills. The emphasis on these sessions would be on fun and indulging in what Marcelo Staricoff refers to as 'the joy of not knowing' (Staricoff, 2020). The community may decide on some rules of play (e.g. timing, interaction patterns, resources) and/or goals (e.g. outcomes, questions, problems) for the creative play time, but other than that the activities would have a strong focus on spontaneity and using methods from games, music, arts and crafts as a lens through which to view problems within a particular discipline. This changing or combining of lenses would involve examining the preconceptions of the subject and asking 'What if...?' questions about other methods for achieving goals within the discipline. It would draw on practice from maker spaces and remixing culture. For example, in computer science, this might involve taking a piece of existing code to play around with and seeing what happens if you add new components or alter elements of the original code. In literature, this might involve rewriting passages from existing texts or playing with generic conventions. In biology, it might involve playing around with elements of an experiment or thinking about how organisms might be different if they were altered in certain ways.

What would learning jamming sessions look like?

The idea of 'jamming' comes from the idea of jazz musicians improvising together and has some similarities with the idea of a 'hackathon', where programmers get together to devise creative solutions to coding problems. The value of jamming sessions and hackathons for promoting creativity in organisations has begun to be explored in the literature (See Belitski & Herzig, 2018 and Briscoe, 2014), with some initial promise, and it is therefore worthwhile for us to sail into the relatively uncharted waters of the affordances these approaches offer for higher education pedagogy.

In learning jamming sessions, communities of tutors and students would get together to 'riff' off each other. The focus would be on experimentation and free expression, where teachers and learners can try out unusual combinations of ideas. It might begin with one person asking a question or proposing an idea. Either as a whole class or in small groups, people from the community would try combining this question or idea with seemingly incongruous concepts, theories or examples in order to generate new solutions or innovative hybrid conceptual structures. This would also be a place to try out different pedagogic approaches – sometimes spontaneous and sometimes planned – testing to see how different combinations of learning activities led to different experiential outcomes. This experiential dimension would be treated with extreme importance at the University, because the positive experience and holistic wellbeing of the community would be a key priority for the institution (Oades, Robinson, Green & Spence, 2014).

What would the character arcs of teachers and learners look like?

A 'character arc' refers to the inner journey or transformation that a character goes through over the course of a story. How would this relate to the experience of staff or students at the University?

The entire learning community of staff, students and other stakeholders would be committed to providing an equitable and empowering experience by creating radically inclusive environments. This type of environment refers to XCa learning community in which all individuals are not only welcomed, but deeply valued, celebrated and engaged in shaping the environment itself. The aim of this would be to ensure that the environment maximally reflected both the diversity of individuals within the University and the wider world beyond it.

Staff would be encouraged to approach their work from a playful perspective and would be supported by their community – including management, colleagues and students – to find joy and fun in their work. This would be supported by the University strategy and policy. All aspects of teaching would place the building of this community, primarily through positive relationships and co-construction of knowledge, at their heart (See Bovill, 2020, Oades, Robinson, Green & Spence, 2014, and Van Schalkwyk & D'Amato, 2015 for inspiration). As such, there would be a shared responsibility to ensure that students would be actively involved in helping to participate in and initiate research projects relevant to the course or department. This may serve to reduce the gap between research and teaching, because the courses themselves would involve co-creating the research that faculty were also pursuing.

For the student, the learning journey would be more joined up, because the whole process of not only their time at the university, but also their life experience before and after, would be viewed in the context of an overarching story. Both students and staff at the University would be encouraged to map this story out as a timeline, character arc or 'river of life', comparing it with models such as Aristotle's concept of *mythos* – the 'organisation of incidents' which have shaped their experience – or Joseph Campbell's concept of the hero's journey, in which each learning episode aligns to a step in the cycle of stepping outside your comfort zone, facing your fears, overcoming struggles and returning changed from the process, only to begin a new adventure (Farmer, 2019).

How can we take learners on a hero's journey that allows them to return home having overcome adversity and brought back the treasure and experiences that they were seeking?

Teaching at the University would be designed to maximise engagement. Effective teaching is highly interactive, but – arguably – the majority of university teaching does not make sufficient effort to engage learners. So how can we make teaching more motivating for learners? We can adapt principles from other modes of communication which have already learned how to engage and entertain people, such as stories and games.

One of the most prevalent models of storytelling is Joseph Cambell's concept of the hero's journey, which synthesised the structure of countless mythological narratives from around the world into a 17-step process of departure, initiation and return. The use of the hero's journey has already been applied to higher education contexts (e.g. Farmer, 2019; Busch, Conrad & Steinicke, 2013) and is part of an evolving tradition of fusing pedagogy and storytelling (Kordaki & Agelidou, 2010; Williams, Cooney & Nelson, 1999). The original model was distilled by Christopher Vogler into a 12-step framework and has been adapted into alternative versions, such as Maureen Murdock's female-centric retelling of the heroine's journey (Murdock, 2020). One of the most recent interpretations of the hero's journey is Dan Harman's story circle. This is one of the simplest versions of the hero's journey and thus one of the easiest to implement. The story circle involves an eight-step cycle in which the protagonist of the story (in this case, the student) goes on a journey from a zone of comfort, to desiring something which forces them to leave their zone of comfort, then attaining the thing they desired, but paying a price, and finally returning to their original starting point having changed. The full list of steps is as follows:

1 They are in a zone of comfort (You).
2 But they want something (Need).
3 They enter an unfamiliar situation (Go).
4 Adapt to it (Search).
5 Get what they wanted (Find).
6 Pay a heavy price (Take).
7 Then return to their familiar situation (Return).
8 Having changed (Change).

In the context of a teaching session, it would be about designing a learning experience which takes the student on this journey. The stages of the session might look something like this.

1 **They are in a zone of comfort (You).** For the first stage, the tutor could begin from what the students already know (their zone of comfort). For example, the tutor may elicit prior knowledge of the topic through a quick poll or quiz or invite playful introductions to the topic through a starter activity which uses images,

analogies or cultural references which anchor the topic in ideas which will be familiar to the learners. They could also introduce a real-life scenario, and a couple of characters, to place the topic in a context.

2 **But they want something (Need).** For the second stage, the tutor could introduce the learning outcomes and what they hope the group – and the individual students within it – will achieve within the session. The tutor may link these to the ultimate learning outcomes of the module or course. The outcomes may be phrased as questions (e.g. 'Can we...?') or using traditional action verbs 'Discuss 2 types of...'. This may be used as an opportunity to encourage learners to reflect: What do we want from this session? What would be a useful output? What is achievable within the constraints that we have?

3 **They enter an unfamiliar situation (Go).** For the third stage, the tutor could introduce some new subject content related to the topic of the session. They would try to present this information in a playful and accessible way, utilising a variety of communicative modes.

4 **Adapt to it (Search).** For the fourth stage, either individually, in pairs or groups, learners actively engage with the subject content. This could be about thinking and writing ideas down, based on analysis or evaluation of the topic. Alternatively, it could involve doing a quick online search for information, looking over the reading they did in preparation for the session to summarise key points, or engaging with the new subject content in an interactive manner.

5 **Get what they wanted (Find).** For the fifth stage, individually, in pairs or groups, learners could try to consolidate their key findings from the activity by producing some notes or other multimedia evidence to share their takeaways with the whole class.

6 **Pay a heavy price (Take).** For the sixth stage, individuals or groups come back together as a whole class and share the summary of their findings. This is also an opportunity to clarify any misconceptions or areas of confusion.

7 **Then return to their familiar situation (Return).** For the seventh stage, the whole class could have the task of thinking about how this learning could be applied to solving real-world, practical problems that learners are likely to face in the near future.

8 **Having changed (Change).** For the final stage, the class reflects on how their understanding has changed and what their key takeaways from the session are. This may also involve thinking about what learners want to know more about, reflecting on changes for future practice or possible avenues for additional research on the topic.

Conclusion

Finally, we have reached the end of the journey. Have we been able to bring back any treasure? This chapter has attempted to paint a picture of a hypothetical institution that truly values active learning, play and storytelling.

The aim of this chapter was to answer three questions:

- What would a university look like if it took active learning seriously?
- What would a university look like if it took play seriously?
- What would a university look like if it took storytelling seriously?

Having explored some of the theory and research in more detail, it seems more evident than ever that current university models do not take these three concepts seriously enough. By allowing existing teacher-centred power structures to perpetuate, universities are – generally unintentionally – creating barriers to learning and social equity.

This chapter clearly has a number of limitations. Firstly, it is just a short flight-of-fancy based on one individual's ideas. It is therefore limited by the positionality of that individual. Although the chapter made use of a range of theory and research, it has not directly tested any of the hypotheses presented.

In future, we need more research evidence on the effectiveness of active learning, play and storytelling in higher education and the evidence needs to be critically evaluated to ascertain whether these ideas can bring genuine value to facilitating the learning process.

We also need more people to contribute their vision of alternative futures for HE. Now that you have been on this journey, it is time for you to take up the mantle of the protagonist. You are invited to write your own reimagining of the university and share this with the author of this chapter and others. You are invited to change education as we know it.

The end? No. It is only the beginning.

References

Abbott, D. (2018, December). Modding tabletop games for education. In: *International Conference on Games and Learning Alliance* (pp. 318–329). Cham: Springer.

Amiryousefi, M. (2015). Individuality in higher education: The use of the multiple-mnemonic method to enhance ESP students' vocabulary development (depth and size) and retention. *Applied Research on English Language, 4(1)*, 45–58.

Belitski, M., & Herzig, M. (2018). The jam session model for group creativity and innovative technology. *The Journal of Technology Transfer, 43(2)*, 506–521.

Betts, T. (2021). *The University of Active Learning, Play and Storytelling*. [Workshop slides] Available at: https://bit.ly/playandstorytelling (Accessed 22 February 2022).

Betts, T. (in press). Story-game based learning. In: *The Active Learning Network 100+ Ideas for Active Learning*.

Biggs, J., & Tang, C. (2011). *Teaching for Quality Learning at University*. London: McGraw-Hill education.

Bovill, C. (2020). Co-creation in learning and teaching: The case for a whole-class approach in higher education. *Higher Education, 79(6)*, 1023–1037.

Briscoe, G. (2014). Digital innovation: The hackathon phenomenon. Creativeworks London/QMUL, London. Available at: http://www.creativeworkslondon.org.uk/wp-content/uploads/2013/11/Digital-Innovation-The-Hackathon-Phenomenon1.pdf (Accessed 23 February 2022).

Busch, C., Conrad, F., & Steinicke, M. (2013). Digital Games and the Hero's Journey in Management Workshops and Tertiary Education. *Electronic journal of e-Learning, 11(1)*, 3–15.

Daniau, S. (2016). The transformative potential of role-playing games: From play skills to human skills. *Simulation & Gaming, 47(4)*, 423–444.

Deslauriers, L., McCarty, L. S., Miller, K., Callaghan, K., & Kestin, G. (2019). Measuring actual learning versus feeling of learning in response to being actively engaged in the classroom. *Proceedings of the National Academy of Sciences, 116(39)*, 19251–19257.

Farmer, R. (2019). The hero's journey in higher education: A twelve stage narrative approach to the design of active, student-centred university modules. *Innovative Practice in Higher Education, 3(3)*, 1–21.

Fischer, B. A. (2019). Fact or fiction? Designing stories for active learning exercises. *Journal of Political Science Education, 15(2)*, 179–190.

Hursen, C., & Fasli, F. G. (2017). Investigating the efficiency of scenario based learning and reflective learning approaches in teacher education. *European Journal of Contemporary Education, 6(2)*, 264–279.

Kordaki, M., & Agelidou, E. (2010). A learning design-based environment for online, collaborative digital storytelling: An example for environmental education. *International Journal of Learning, 17(5)*, 95–106.

Lean, J., Illingworth, S., & Wake, P. (2018). Unhappy families: Using tabletop games as a technology to understand play in education. *Research in Learning Technology, 26*, 1–13.

Malone, T. W. (1981). Toward a theory of intrinsically motivating instruction. *Cognitive Science, 5(4)*, 333–369.

Malone, T. W., & Lepper, M. R. (2021). Making learning fun: A taxonomy of intrinsic motivations for learning. In *Aptitude, Learning, and Instruction* (pp. 223–254). London: Routledge.

Moulton, S. T. (2014). Applying psychological science to higher education: Key findings and open questions. *Perspectives on Psychological Science, 1*, 181–210.

Murdock, M. (2020). *The Heroine's Journey: Woman's Quest for Wholeness.* Boulder: Shambhala Publications.

Oades, L. G., Robinson, P., Green, S., & Spence, G. B. (2014). Towards a positive university. In: *Positive Psychology in Higher Education* (pp. 15–22). London: Routledge.

Pipkin, E. (2019). *The Ground Itself* [Game] Available at: https://everestpipkin.itch.io/the-ground-itself (Accessed 23 February 2022).

Race, P. (2019). *The Lecturer's Toolkit: A Practical Quide to Assessment, Learning and Teaching.* London: Routledge.

Sidhu, P., & Carter, M. (2021). Exploring the resurgence and educative potential of 'dungeons and dragons'. *Scan: The Journal for Educators, 40(6)*, 12–16.

Sidhu, P., Carter, M., & Curwood, J. S. (2021). *Unlearning in games: Deconstructing failure in Dungeons & Dragons.* Proceedings of DiGRA Australia 2021, 1–4.

Staricoff, M. (2020). *The Joy of Not Knowing: A Philosophy of Education Transforming Teaching, Thinking, Learning and Leadership in Schools.* London: Routledge.

Van Schalkwyk, G. J., & D'Amato, R. C. (Eds.). (2015). *Facilitative Collaborative Knowledge Co-construction: New Directions for Teaching and Learning, Number 143.* New York: John Wiley & Sons.

Wang, S. H. (2021, January). The application of information processing theory in higher education. In: *2021 2nd International Conference on Education, Knowledge and Information Management (ICEKIM)* (pp. 930–933). IEEE.

Williams, K. C., Cooney, M., & Nelson, J. (1999). Storytelling and storyacting as an active learning strategy. *Journal of Early Childhood Teacher Education, 20(3)*, 347–352.

Tang, G., & Yuen, R. H. Y. (2016). Hong Kong as the 'neoliberal exception' of China: Transformation of Hong Kong citizenship before and after the transfer of sovereignty. *Journal of Chinese Political Science, 21(4)*, 469–484.

Zhang, L., & Shang, J. (2015, July). How video games enhance learning: A discussion of James Paul Gee's views in his book what video games have to teach us about learning and literacy. In *International Conference on Hybrid Learning and Continuing Education* (pp. 404–411). Cham: Springer.

2 Play not tell

Agency and becoming in the playful university

Roy Hanney

Introduction

There is an old screenwriting maxim: show not tell. The principle here is to avoid exposition, to focus on telling a story using audio visual language. In doing so you avoid lazy writing that does all the work, explains everything in lengthy monologues and dead dialogue. It gives agency to the audience; it gets them to do the work. It doesn't fill in the gaps, instead it leaves them wide open for exploration. It places the audience as co-creator with the writer/director since they will have to puzzle through the motifs, metaphors, allegories and mise-en-scène to make sense of the narrative. Show not tell is a call to a form of active audience agency that is echoed in this chapter's call to action which asks how play might be employed as an active learning strategy to promote agency and autonomy in our learners.

Challenges

My own personal interest in play emerges from a reflection on several challenges faced by media practice educators. In particular, how best to promote creativity among undergraduate students especially during the early, ideation phase of their project work. Students tend to race to the end of a project and don't value the ideation phase of project development. Consequently, their ideas are often poorly conceived and suffer from what gestalt psychologists call 'experience bias', sometimes referred to as 'functional fixedness'. A cognitive bias can sometimes prevent us from coming up with novel or creative solutions to creative problems. Instead, we fixate on the familiar and find it hard to think 'outside-the-box'.

In addition, there is an ongoing need to articulate the way in which critical thinking manifests within creative practice. In part, because

DOI: 10.4324/9781003360032-3

to be able to speak it means we are better placed to design teaching strategies to promote it. But also, because, as practice educators, we need to be able to defend our subject discipline against criticisms that media practice is not academic. The theory-practice nexus is difficult to untangle but it is important we attempt to do so.

Then there is the feeling that when engaged in the early stages of a creative process the creator is 'scratching away' at something, that there is a revelatory process at work. Michelangelo is often quoted as saying that "every block of stone has a statue inside it, and it is the task of the sculptor to discover it" (possibly an internet meme rather than an actual quote). There is a resonance here with the notion that the creative idea is shaped by the milieu, the context, the debate, it is embedded within an assemblage of concepts, traditions, and practices. The role of the creative is to reveal, shape and bring into being form through a kind of archaeological exploration. It is the creator's tacit intuition that often leads the inquiry in one direction or another and this is another of the key challenges for creative practice educators. How on earth do you teach tacit intuition?

A possible solution

The answer to these challenges is fairly simple once you get to it. You do it by adopting 'playfulness' as an active learning strategy. There is a growing body of literature on this topic, drawing from research into early years development, evolutionary theory, pedagogy and philosophy. The basic premise is that everything we learn from an early age, we learn through play, that this is the primary mode through which we discover the world. But, as argued below, play doesn't just promote physical skills, it is also the principal way in which we develop our creative and critical faculties. It is through the repetitious practice of play that we develop, our tacit and intuitive capacities. The activity of play gives us strategies for exploring what is possible, it helps us with ideation since it gives us permission to experiment. It structures a liminal space between rational and pre-rational thinking in which the theory-practice nexus resides. It offers a methodology that is at once revelatory and places tacit intuition at the heart of the creative process.

Learner agency, autonomy, and the neuroscience of play

In the case of higher education, agency refers to "the capacity to act in the world" (Larsen-Freeman 2019). I would argue that even more than that, agency comes about when learner's take a position in relation to the world. Agency is essentially dialogic; it is fundamentally creative and evolves through responses to problem encounters. Implicit within the notion of agency is the possibility for transformation and thus any pedagogy that promotes agency is surely also a pedagogy of becoming. We don't exist passively in the world, adapting to events as they pass us by; "we create and dwell in a world" (Joseph AN 2017, p. 24). Approaches to learning and teaching that embrace this philosophy are typified by exploration, openness, non-judgemental acceptance, improvisation, ownership, problem-solving, risk-taking, co-construction and collaboration (Cremin & Chappel 2021). They scaffold a bounded play-space where purposeful and responsive thought co-constructs knowledge, understanding and appreciation of the world. What occurs in such a space is "joint attention" (Joseph AN 2017, p. 8) through a shared, participatory encounter that is truly inter-subjective.

It has been argued by Boyd (2009) that activities which promote joint attention are adaptive evolutionary strategies. They serve as a "stimulus and training for a flexible mind" (Boyd 2009, p. 86) in a similar way that physical activities such as wrestling, running, and hide and seek provide opportunities to rehearse behaviours that would enhance the potential for survival. This kind of physical play provides a means for rehearsing possible future encounters and therefore survival of the individual, the group, the species. In a similar way, play promotes mental activities that train the mind for encounters beyond the here and now. Boyd (2009, p. 88) argues that play is an evolutionary adaptation that enables human beings to respond to dynamic information flows, to make decisions that impact directly on survival. The ability to analyse, evaluate and synthesise information, be it social, environmental, physical or affective, impacts directly on a species capability for survival. A compelling argument in support of this position is the fact that we, as a species expend quite so much time, effort and energy in such a highly motivated activity that would, in the savannah of our origins, have resulted in a high risk of predation. Boyd suggests that consequently play must serve an important and powerful function beyond that of the obvious immediate rewards. Think about how we develop skills for flight and fight, recovery and balance, cooperation and strategy in children's play. These are essential survival skillsets in the savannah.

Play as pedagogic strategy

Play is characterised by purposiveness, openness, free expression, boundedness (in time and place). The play-space is a conceptual, imagined space in which experimentation can occur. Play is immersive and collaborative, interaction and co-construction are the primary constitutive elements of play (Joseph AN 2017, p. 23). We have a compulsion to play, it is something that comes naturally to us, and it is something we enjoy for its own sake. Surely, if play is such a powerful and compelling driver for participation in activities that offer the opportunity to explore problems, try out different solutions and engage with a full range of possibilities (Smith 2019, p. 61), then there must be a benefit to adopting play as a pedagogic approach.

The evidence from neuroscience suggests that play encourages the growth of more neural tissue. Play, we are told "enhances neural plasticity, intellectual dexterity, adaptability, emotional learning and resilience to depression" (Nørgärd 2021, p. 151). Psychologists also tell us that play correlates with all sorts of positive cognitive attributes including non-linear, divergent and imaginative thinking (Loudon 2019, p. 69). Capabilities that correlate with creativity and innovation which are highly sought-after employability skills. In addition, we are told that play stimulates the brain to release dopamine, a powerful reward stimulus that motivates us to repeatedly engage in play. Smith (2019) explains that though we recognise the value and importance of play to young children. At around the age of five, we are expected to abandon play for more serious learning. Smith argues that play is a serious business at any age and challenges the assumption that play is only of value in early years teaching. The importance of play in knowledge construction is clearly set out in developmental psychology. Very young children engage in exploration, solve problems, conceptualise and make decisions based on evidence that is generated through play (Smith 2019, p. 58). Through play they acquire knowledge about the world, explore the world, interpret the world leading to the creation of novel ideas. Their play is analytic, evaluative and leads to synthesis. Furthermore, Smith (2019) evidences the way in which play-based learning shares common characteristics with the process of academic research: knowledge construction, problem solving, evidence-based decision making and so on. So why do we abandon it as a pedagogy early in the educational journey? Surely, we should embrace it!

But we need to be careful with our terminology and ensure we are clear about "what play is and what play isn't" (James 2019, p. 3). For example, many have argued that there is an important difference between games and play. Boyd recognises play as a "mutually amplifying" (Boyd 2009), open ended, cooperative zero-sum game, i.e. in which nobody wins or loses. Whereas games are structured, task orientated, goal focused and competitive (James 2019, 7). For Nørgärd (2021), games reflect the metric-driven ecology of higher education. Where the focus is on quantifiable performance and extrinsic rewards thereby accentuating "a culture of competition and performance" (Nørgärd 2021, p. 142). Games encourage students to "do education" (Nørgärd 2021, p. 142) since there is no incentive to be playful, to take risks, to be exploratory or to celebrate failure and thus to embrace limitless possibilities. In a similar fashion, James (2019) argues that creativity and play should be thought of as separate and at times antithetical categories (James 2019, p. 7). Creativity we are told is driven by a need for outcomes while play is exploratory. Play is removed from the everyday, it doesn't satisfy the need for food clothes and shelter, it's for-the-sake-of-which is entirely abstracted from the practice of the everyday. Nevertheless James (2019) challenges us to resist definitions and typologies lest it constrain us, and we get lost in trying to pin down the idea and wrap ourselves in superficial analysis. Play is an attitude, a mindset, it is anything that is exploratory, open ended and is entirely subjective. It is about giving yourself up to the moment, allowing the encounter to be the experience from which you learn. James argues that this mind set better prepares students for uncertain, messy encounters in the real world (James 2019, 12).

The playful university – Welcome to the mind gym

Though still difficult to define and much contested as a concept, the idea of the playful university is clearly a well-established and well-documented phenomenon. There are annual conferences, jams, books, articles, manifestos and even a regular magazine (cf. creativeacademic.uk for Exploring Play in HE). Nevertheless, we must consider the possibility that "playful higher education lacks [a] robust theoretical and conceptual foundation" (Nørgärd 2021, p. 143). In an attempt to address this gap in our theoretical understanding, Nørgärd posits a theoretical framework which addresses some of the definitional problems in the field. In particular, Nørgärd is concerned to separate the concept of play from that of playfulness suggesting that it is the later quality that we should be aiming to promote, that play, in and of itself, is not the ambition of the playful university.

The autotelic (Nørgärd 2021, p. 144) nature of play means that it is intention-less. In other words, the for-the-sake-of-which of play is nothing more than play, it exists for its own purposes. That while there may be consequences, outputs or actions that arise from play, these are not intrinsically the purpose of the play. However, in higher education there is a requirement for intentionality. A drive towards knowledge acquisition, development of competencies for employment, values, and beliefs (Nørgärd 2021, p. 145). Unless we wish to abolish the intentionality that underpins the educational project then we will need to find a way to resolve what Nørgärd sees as competing tension between play and education. Actually, we can resolve this tension simply by adopting a playful mind set in which we become playful and occupy ourselves with playfulness. It is this playful attitude that we need to take hold of or allow to take hold of us. We can do this in a way that allows us to respect the goals and intentions of higher education but preserve the spirit, the attitude of the playful mindset. In this sense the for-the-sake-of-which of playfulness is no longer autotelic (i.e. lacking intention), it can be purposeful, undertaken with intent and goal orientated. Yet it retains the possibility for the open ended, exploratory, messy, uncertain, risky characteristics of play.

However, Nørgärd cautions that we should remain starkly critical of approaches which seem playful but in fact are just gamified activities. Pedagogies that wear an illusory mask of playfulness but are typified by gaming and gamification (Nørgärd 2021, p. 146) are counterproductive and will reproduce the metric driven 'doing' of education typified by the neo-liberal university model. If we seek to promote learner agency, autonomy, and a becoming pedagogy then arguably we should steer away from the kind of activities that merely construct a *playpen* rather than provide a *playground*. Instead, we might imagine our learning spaces as *mind-gyms* in which we train for higher intellectual capabilities. In the same way that elite athletes train for gold medals we should seek out the science of learner agency and design learning experiences that work on the muscles of the brain, that grow new neural pathways and develop those critical and intellectual capabilities that will equip our students for the future. Such a space might embrace Nørgärd's three principles for playful learning:

- *The Exploratorium*: a playful space in which students can be curious take risks, explore alternatives, ask what-if questions and wonder about the world (Nørgärd 2021, p. 146).
- *The Experimentarium*: an unbounded space in which students can "experiment with themselves, knowledge and the world" (Nørgärd 2021, p. 148).
- *The Collaboratorium*: a shared space where people have "care and concern" (Nørgärd 2021, p. 150) towards each other and form an empathetic cooperative which is intensely social and inherently interpersonal.

We might think of the *mind-gym* as a becoming space where transformation can occur. It is a space that celebrates divergent thinking and offers opportunities to practice thinking differently and embracing the novel. Where impossibilities can be imagined, boundaries crossed, and the world turned upside down. Importantly it is a safe place to take risks.

Conclusion

A playful pedagogy is focused on transformation. It is a becoming pedagogy. It is social, collaborative and celebrates co-construction as means for "training for the unexpected" (Vandervert 2017, p. 208) and for the development of capabilities for "the skilful manipulation of ideas" (Vandervert 2017, p. 208). Acting out, rehearsing, experimenting by taking on different roles, not by being me but by becoming someone else. These are the kind of qualities that give our students permission to be risk takers and ultimately to break down what they know, rearrange it and create new ideas (critical thinking = analysis, evaluation, and synthesis). Playfulness is highly purposeful, though it is not action towards specific goals, instead it is about generating limitless possibilities (Loudon 2019, p. 68). Through playfulness socialisation occurs as one person enlists help from another to solve a problem or to achieve other goals (Vandervert 2017, p. 214). Playfulness promotes a curiosity for what is not known, or not apparent and a realisation that reason logic and structured thinking may not be on its own enough to reveal what is hidden from us. It ferments a non-judgemental mindset that would help break free of experiential bias that traps us into functional fixedness when ideating, creating and innovating. The playful university is a liminal space in which critical thinking is employed as a tool for discovery and exploration.

If we can embrace these ideas then perhaps, we can collectively work towards turning our classrooms into an *Exploratorium, a Experimentarium* and/or a *Collaboratorium*. Perhaps this is a model for a playful university in anthesis to that of the neo-liberal model in which students 'do' education. Perhaps it is time to rethink what universities are for and to embrace a new way of doing things.

References

Boyd, B. (2009). *On the Origin of Stories: Evolution, Cognition, and Fiction.* Cambridge, MA: Harvard University Press.

Cremin, T. and Chappell, K. (2021). Creative pedagogies: a systematic review. *Research Papers in Education, 36(3),* 299–331.

James, A. (2019). Making the case for the Playful University. In: A. James and C. Nerantzi, (Eds.) *The Power of Play in Higher Education.* London: Palgrave Macmillan, pp.1–19.

Joseph AN, C. (2018). On learning, playfulness, and becoming human. *Philosophy, 93(1),* 3–29.

Loudon, G. (2019). Exploration: experiences of running a 'play and creativity' module in a school of art & design. In: A. James and C. Nerantzi, (Eds.) *The Power of Play in Higher Education*. London: Palgrave Macmillan, pp.67–74.

Larsen-Freeman, D. (2019). On language learner agency: a complex dynamic systems theory perspective. *The Modern Language Journal, 103*, 61–79

Nørgärd, R.T. (2021). Philosophy for the playful university – towards a theoretical foundation for playful higher education. In: S.S.E. Bengsten, S. Robinson and W. Shumar, (Eds.) *The University Becoming: Perspectives from Philosophy and Social Theory*. Cham: Springer International Publishing, pp.141–156.

Smith, S., (2019). Exploration: Play in practice—innovation through play in the postgraduate curriculum. In: A. James and C. Nerantzi, (Eds.) *The Power of Play in Higher Education*. London: Palgrave Macmillan, pp.57–66.

Vandervert, L. (2017). Vygotsky meets neuroscience: the cerebellum and the rise of culture through play. *American Journal of Play, 9(2),* 202–227.

3 Bricolage as a holistic model for active learning

Sarah Honeychurch

In this chapter, I will paint a picture of active learning that I think helps to address three well-known educational issues: the stress of assessment for learners, the pressures of excessive marking workloads for staff and the fact that many learners (particularly the ones who need it most) do not engage in 'formative' activities unless they have a grade attached to them. The practice that I will describe is called bricolage (and is based on the writings of Seymour Papert), the socio-cultural structure that supports it is based on the affinity spaces of John Paul Gee, and the model of assessment is called patchwork text. The picture of teaching and learning that emerges from this is a holistic structure that is academically rigorous where both learners and educators can work authentically and even enjoy teaching and learning together.

As educators, we know that the process of learning is usually more important than any product of learning, and that what we hope to do when we engage learners in active learning is to help them to develop attitudes towards learning that are transferrable beyond a particular context. I suggest that in order to help learners to develop their own supportive structures we should focus on helping them to develop appropriate practices rather than just helping them to form short-lived groups or communities (I say short-lived here in recognition that many educators are looking at using active learning in their particular unit, module or course, rather than having a focus at a programmatic level). We might think of active learning in terms of helping learners to develop transferable skills, we might even frame this in terms of graduate attributes and employability if that language resonates with our learners/audience. We might think about it as helping to develop the skills and knowledge appropriate for a cohort/subject, or we might talk in terms of building learner trust and confidence. I think that all of these are appropriate ways of describing the goals of active learning, and they are all aims that we would hope to achieve.

We are often told that modern learners are digital natives because they have grown up immersed in a digital world, for example, Prensky thought that learners who had grown up steeped in digital media would find it easy to use any technology (Prensky, 2001). However, as Bennett et al. caution, we should be wary of making generalisations about the capability of a whole generation of learners, not least because Prensky's original assertions were based on "anecdotes and appeals to common-sense beliefs" and might not apply to all learners (Bennett, Mahon and Kervin, 2008, p. 777). What is apparent from this more recent literature is that while there are high levels of *ownership* of computers and mobile phones, only a minority of learners are digital *creators* (Kvavik, Caruso and Morgan, 2004, cited in Bennett et al., 2008, p. 778). However, although modern learners are not, for the most part, digital natives in Prensky's sense, they are comfortable *using* social media. With this qualification, I suggest that looking at how adolescents behave on social media can give us insights. In particular, this can be helpful in thinking about how to structure active learning that encourages learners to transfer practices from their personal lives into their academic studies. Mimi Ito has conducted a considerable body of research into this exact area.

Ito describes the behaviour of adolescents engaging with each other via social media as "Hanging Out, Messing Around, Geeking Out" (HOMAGO) (Ito, 2010). She suggests that this behaviour is best understood as a self-directed structure of experiential learning that can support informal, peer-led learning structures and that also describes how these adolescents learn in new and social media environments (Ito, 2010; 2019). "Hanging out" consists in activities such as using (viewing) YouTube, posting to Facebook and text messaging, which is a fairly passive activity. This passive behaviour can, in time, lead to the more active behaviours of "messing around", which Ito defines as a sort of "tinkering", and "geeking out", which involves taking an even deeper dive into the practices. To give an example: hanging out could involve a learner posting to social media a gif that they have found online; messing around could be a learner making a gif for themselves by using an online gif maker, while geeking out could be a learner creating a gif from scratch using their own images and photo-editing software.

Bennett et al.'s findings have important similarities with Ito's research into HOMAGO. Ito shows that while the majority of youths are happy to "hang out" (that is, to consume) online, a minority also have or develop the digital skills needed to "mess around" or "geek out": that is, to use social media in order to create and remix artefacts (Ito, 2010; 2019). The challenge is to move learners from the fairly passive "hanging out" to the very active "geeking out". One way we might help learners to make this transition is by designing active learning that uses the social-constructionist practice that Seymour Papert calls bricolage (Papert, 1993), and which corresponds to the practice that Ito describes as "messing around".

Bricolage comes from the French verb 'bricoler', which translates as "to tinker", or "improvise" (Baldick, 2008, n.p.). Papert introduces us to the term bricolage in order to compare and contrast two approaches to learning, which we might broadly call the theoretical and the practical. In bricolage, learners solve problems not by learning about a theoretical approach and applying it, but by actively playing around with concepts and artefacts and seeing what happens (Turkle and Papert, 1991). Bricolage is a model of learning, teaching and assessment that is iterative: a learner produces an original artefact, shares it with their learning community at an early stage to receive feedback about it, and then uses this feedback to refine and resubmit their artefact. By doing this, learners use their existing knowledge and build upon and consolidate that knowledge by playing around and sharing the results with their peers in a low-risk setting (Papert, 1993). Educators are on hand to step in if peer feedback is inappropriate (for example, to correct a misunderstanding), or to endorse particularly helpful instances of feedback, but they do not typically give detailed feedback themselves. This is therefore a model in which learners receive rich feedback as and when they need it, but without causing a large marking workload for educators.

The theory of learning that underpins the practice of bricolage is called social constructionism, which is a theory of learning that emphasises the importance of learners constructing their own knowledge (Papert, 1993; Turkle and Papert, 1991). It is similar to the more well-known theory of knowledge called social constructivism in that both view learning as the building of knowledge structures, but constructionism puts more emphasis on the importance to learning of 'hands-on' knowledge making with and for other learners and is thus more situated and pragmatic (Ackermann, 2001). Constructionism has been described as being 'learning through social making', though Papert rejects this definition as being too simplistic. Berland offers a fuller explanation of why this type of activity leads to meaningful learning: it is because learners *create personal meaning* when they construct working artefacts with and for a community (Berland, 2017, my emphasis).

One thing that makes this model of learning so powerful is the serendipitous emergence that it enables. Implicit in bricolage is the thought that we can learn when things don't go as planned (some people call this failure, but I prefer to avoid that particular word in this context as it implies that things have gone wrong). Constructionism emphasises the serendipity of active learning: attempts to create artefacts that do not initially work can provide information to the maker that helps them to better understand the problem they are trying to solve, and to produce another version of the artefact (Papert calls this 'rapid feedback'). Making a tangible artefact and sharing it with one's learning community can be particularly useful for a learner when things do not work because others can test it and help the learner to understand what is going 'wrong' and why. This highlights the importance of designing teaching and assessment that gives learners opportunities to submit their work for informal review before it undergoes final 'high-stakes' assessment.

The picture that I am sketching here is of a holistic picture of learning and assessment – where learners produce early versions of their artefacts and share them with their learning community (this could be a small group, or a large cohort), and give and receive feedback with those peers. Eventually, some of these artefacts can be (re)submitted for formal (summative) marking, and by the time this happens learners will have gained confidence in what they are doing because they have had constructive feedback and also – importantly – they have had time to assimilate this feedback into future iterations of their work. This helps to remove the uncertainty of assessment from learners, and thus can reduce the stress that they experience without adding to the marking workload of the educator.

Although this type of active learning might just seem like fun (and, as those of us who do or support this type of learning know, it *is* a lot of fun), when properly designed and scaffolded it can also lead to deep, meaningful learning. I want to emphasise this point – to the uninitiated it might seem that bricolage is unstructured play, and that there is no active role for the educator, or that all types of games and play will lead to meaningful and relevant learning. This view can lead to various problems: such as learners not taking the activity seriously as it is not 'real' learning, or other educators trying to copy a learning design and missing out a vital part because it does not seem to them to be important. This is why, for me, theory and practice must go hand in hand – it is vital to both know *what* works and *why* it works. I hope that this chapter has gone some way towards explaining this.

I wrote earlier about the challenges of ensuring that learners engage with activities that we know will help them but that they do not see as being important. In this next section I want to address this. First, I reiterate my comment about it not being sufficient to just put learners into active learning groups, but that instead the focus should be on helping them to develop appropriate practices such as bricolage. I would further emphasise that it is also not sufficient just to give learners an activity (such as asking them to post to a VLE Forum), educators also need to put in some scaffolding to support learners and to help them to appreciate the relevance of what we ask them to do. The structure of the space we provide is important to enable all of this, and here I am not referring to the physical organisation of a space, but to its underlying ethos.

The structure that I suggest to underpin all of this is based on the affinity spaces of Gee (Gee, 2004), which is developed as an adaptation of the community of practice (CoP) of Lave and Wenger (1991). The term CoP was originally devised by Lave and Wenger to describe how situated learning happens when a group of people come together because of common interests, goals, or knowledge, and collaborate and interact with each other (Lave and Wenger, 1991). In this model, experts work in the middle of the community while novices watch from the periphery, gradually being drawn into the centre as they gain experience and expertise. Gee outlines his concept of an affinity space to update this model for a modern, more participatory, settings where relationships are not so rigidly hierarchical, such as online games.

Affinity spaces are similar to CoPs in that they both contain groups of people with common interests. However, in an affinity space members are not separated according to their level of experience – any learner can practice in the centre or sit on the periphery depending on how they are feeling at the time (Gee, 2004). In these spaces the same individual can be both novice with regard to some aspects and expert with regard to others. Learners with a range of abilities can thus occupy the same space – some actively working and others lurking – and those who need feedback can quickly find someone to provide it for them and feel confident that the educator will step in if need be. This will go some way towards ensuring that learners will engage with 'formative' activities because they appreciate the immediate relevance of so doing. If we want, we can go one stage further and embed summative assessment into the active learning design.

I wrote above about how in bricolage learners give and receive feedback from each other, which is of course a type of peer review. Peer review is a well-known model in higher education (Nicol, Thomson and Breslin, 2014; Topping, 2005), so this gives a place to start that is not too far away from current practices. However, while peer review is a powerful model of formative feedback, I think that there are good reasons for suggesting that the educator determines the final mark.

There is already model of assessment which is highly applicable here, and that is Patchwork Text:

> A Patchwork Text is basically a composite piece of writing created from several shorter, separate pieces written beforehand, the 'patches'. It ... [is] an innovative kind of assessment in which the character of the main or only assignment of a module is modified by being produced cumulatively and by containing different components.
>
> (Ovens, 2003, p. 109)

In this learning design, learners are given small pieces of work to produce, making it a perfect model to assess learning built on bricolage. These pieces are given formative feedback by peers, and optionally by the educator as well. At the end of the year, course or module, learners select a pre-agreed number of these formative assignments (patches) and submit them for formal assessment (reworking them if they wish) with a reflective piece which stitches the patches together and explains why each patch has been chosen. This portfolio is then marked by the educator. Patchwork Text is traditionally used in the context of individual assessment, but I think this could be easily extended to assess group work and to turn the process into a creative and playful one – both for educators and for learners.

I hope that you have enjoyed reading my picture of holistic active learning using bricolage. As I think that I have shown, when properly structured this model of active learning can help to alleviate the stress that learners experience during assessment due to a lack of confidence in their abilities and uncertainty about the quality of their work. It also allows learners to receive the feedback they need at the time that they need it without causing excessive marking workloads for educators. The outcome is an environment in which learners engage in meaningful learning because they see the relevance of the learning activities they are provided with, rather than (just) because they will be given a mark for their work, and both educators and learners enjoy the experience.

References

Ackermann, E. (2001, January). *Piaget's Constructivism, Papert's Constructionism: What's the Difference?* https://www.researchgate.net/publication/238495459_Piaget's_Constructivism_Papert's_Constructionism_What's_the_difference

Baldick, C. (2008). *The Oxford Dictionary of Literary Terms* (3rd ed.). Oxford University Press. https://doi.org/10.1093/acref/9780199208272.001.0001

Bennett, S., Maton, K., & Kervin, L. (2008). The 'digital natives' debate: A critical review of the evidence. *British Journal of Educational Technology*, *39*(5), 775–786. https://doi.org/10.1111/j.1467-8535.2007.00793.x

Berland, M. (2017). Constructionist Learning. In *SAGE Encyclopedia of Out of School Learning*.

Gee, J. P. (2004). *Situated Language and Learning: A Critique of Traditional Schooling* (Reprinted). Routledge.

Ito, M. (Ed.). (2010). *Hanging out, Messing Around, and Geeking out: Kids Living and Learning with New Media*. MIT Press.

Ito, M. (Ed.). (2019). *Affinity Online: How Connection and Shared Interest Fuel Learning*. New York University Press.

Kvavik, R. B., Caruso, J. B., & Morgan, G. (2004). ECAR study of students and information technology2004: convenience, connection, and control. Boulder, CO: EDUCAUSE Center for Applied Research. Retrieved April 12, 2021, from http://www.educause.edu/ir/library/pdf/ers0405/rs/ers0405w.pdf

Lave, J., & Wenger, E. (1991). *Situated Learning: Legitimate Peripheral Participation*. Cambridge University Press.

Nicol, D., Thomson, A., & Breslin, C. (2014). Rethinking feedback practices in higher education: a peer review perspective. *Assessment & Evaluation in Higher Education*, *39*(1), 102–122. doi: 10.1080/02602938.2013.795518.

Ovens, P. (2003). Editorial. *Innovations in Education and Teaching International*, *40*(2), 109–111. https://doi.org/10.1080/1470329031000088969

Papert, S. (1993). *Mindstorms: Children, Computers, and Powerful Ideas* (2nd ed). Basic Books.

Prensky, M. (2001). Digital natives, digital immigrants part 1. *On the Horizon*, *9*(5), 1–6. https://doi.org/10.1108/10748120110424816

Topping, K. J. (2005). Trends in peer learning. *Educational Psychology*, *25*(6), 631–645. https://doi.org/10.1080/01443410500345172.

Turkle, S., & Papert, S. (1991). *Epistemological Pluralism and the Revaluation of the Concrete*. (p. 191). Ablex Publishing.

4 The role of active learning in transformative learning and teaching experiences

Christina Magkoufopoulou

Introduction

The Higher Education (HE) landscape is constantly changing and transforming to meet the needs of the ever-evolving student population and of the ever-changing work sector. Some of the major changes that HE has undergone over the past decades include the massification of Higher Education, that resulted in a diversified student population (Evans et al., 2021), as well as the constantly increasing use of technology to facilitate learning, teaching and assessment (Chauhan et al., 2021). The literature also reveals a major shift of the purpose and aims of HE towards providing an 'employable workforce' through the development of relevant attributes and skills needed for future employment (Wong et al., 2021). But the expectations and desires of prospective employers are also in constant change; with reports showing the need for reskilling of 50% of the employees (World Economic Forum, 2016, 2020). While active learning as a skill has maintained its place in the top skills required by employers during the 4th industrial revolution, we can see that other skills, such as resource management and the ability to train others, have disappeared from the desired top 15 skills for 2025, whereas others such as innovation, resilience and stress tolerance were added to the list (World Economic Forum, 2016, 2020).

Central to this transforming landscape of education and employment, and of equal importance, we can find both the students and the educators that have to adapt their learning and teaching practices, respectively, to navigate those continuously changing environments. To accommodate these changes, additional "multilevel interventions" for lecturers are put in place in HE (Abd Rahman et al., 2020, p. 51). This further highlights the need of academics to frequently transform their understanding of their role and their identity, that is unstable

DOI: 10.4324/9781003360032-5

Active learning in transformative learning and teaching experiences 35

and ephemeral (Watermeyer & Tomlinson, 2022), in relation to their students and HE requirements. In this process the educators also become learners that need to learn new, and frequently ill-defined, ways to perform their jobs. As Yrjö Engeström (2001) presents it very clearly "People and organizations are all the time learning something that is not stable, not even defined or understood ahead of time. In important transformations of our personal lives and organizational practices, we must learn new forms of activity which are not yet there." This raises the question if we are to learn something that is not there, what is it that we are learning? An intuitive answer here would be that, in order to adapt our learning to unstable knowledge and situations, we need to learn how to learn and teach our students to do that as well (McGuire & McGuire, 2015). To that end, we need to be open to transformation and able to adjust and transform our understanding of the world and our position in it.

In this chapter, I will endeavour to analyse the central role that transformation plays in learning through an exploration of a selection of learning theories (and not an exhaustive list of all the learning theories) and how they define learning. Through this exploration I will endeavour to identify what constitutes transformative learning experiences and what are the required conditions for transformation to occur, as well as how this is inherently linked with active learning principles. In this chapter, it would become evident that active learning is the cornerstone of transformational learning and teaching experiences and how by bearing that in mind we can create a framework for transformative active learning.

A theoretical exploration of transformative learning

As the main focus of this chapter is to explore the role of active learning within transformative learning experiences, I must start by introducing the transformative learning theory (Mezirow, 1978). Transformative learning theory is primarily an adult learning theory that originated from studies focusing on women re-entering education in the 70s in the United States. However, it can be applied in the whole lifespan of learners (Kegan, 2009) and can also find its place within HE (Raikou & Karalis, 2016). Transformative learning theory recognises the importance of past experiences and assumptions held by the learners and how these frame their worldview and self-conception. Mezirow refers to these as "meaning perspectives" (Mezirow, 1978) or "frames of reference" (Mezirow, 1981)[1]. Transformative learning theory emphasises that for transformative learning to occur the existing (problematic) frames of references need to be transformed "to make them more inclusive, discriminating, open, reflective and emotionally able to change" (Mezirow, 2006, p. 26).

Transformative learning theory finds its foundations in Habermas' instrumental and communicative learning (Habermas, 1981). According to Mezirow (2006) the distinction between instrumental learning and communicative learning lies within the functionality of learning. In instrumental learning, the purpose is to assess a truth claim, and it can be applied in situations that can be empirically validated. On the contrary, communicative learning occurs through discourse and aims to reach a *best judgement*. In communicative learning, discourse aims to lead to a consensus amongst equal, free[2], well-informed, open to other ideas, self-aware and capable of self-reflection learners. For transformative learning to occur in both instrumental and communicative learning, critical reflection is required. Critical reflection of our own and that of others' "source, nature and consequences of assumptions" is the first step to the transformative learning process (Mezirow, 2006, p. 27). It is only after the critical reflection that we can determine if something is true (instrumental learning) or arrive in more justified beliefs through discourse (communicative learning), before we can take action to transform our perspective, and frames of reference. Hence, Mezirow's theory is centred around the role of discourse and how discourse can shape one's perception by allowing individuals to become aware of other ways of making sense of the world (Gouthro, 2006). The educators are therefore challenged to create the dialogical environment (Gouthro, 2006) that will enable critical reflection but also ensure that the learning environment allows the learners to meet the conditions for being able to fully and freely participate in critical reflective discourse.

According to Kegan, the frame of reference at its heart is a way of knowing, and to that extent transformational learning should refer to an epistemological change rather than just a change in behaviour or quantity of knowledge. For educators to further facilitate transformative learning, Kegan (2009) advises to turn to constructive-developmental theory and to that extend, advises that educators need to fully understand the current and pre-existing frames of reference and epistemologies of their learners, the history of prior transformations that the learners have undergone, as well as the epistemological complexity of the present learning challenges that the learners experience. As Kegan (2009, p. 46) states "this transformation will be better understood and facilitated if its history is better honored and its future better appreciated". It is very much possible that learning can still take place without changes of the existing frames of references, if the newly presented knowledge or acquired experience fits perfectly within the existing frames of reference. Such learning constitutes *informative learning*, which can still be a valuable learning experience (Kegan, 2009). In that case, without transformation, learning reinforces the existing frame of reference. Frequently active learning strategies are used to facilitate informative learning, such as hands-on experiences, group-work, discussions and so forth. This could be referred to as *informative active learning* that will allow the learner to acquire new knowledge, skills and attributes that fit with the existing frames of references and hence do not lead to a transformative learning experience. When new ideas do not fit with our existing frames of reference, they are often quickly rejected. This further highlights the importance of critical reflection and active engagement in discourse for transformation to occur.

Another theory that is centred around reflection that can lead to transformation is Kolb's experiential learning theory, where transforming experiences are a result of reflective observation and active experimentation. Kolb defines learning as "the process whereby knowledge is created through the transformation of experience. Knowledge results from the combination of grasping and transforming experience" (Passarelli & Kolb, 2012); where grasping experience refers to acquiring new information, and transforming experience to the interpretation of this information (reflective observation) and consequent action as a result of this information (active experimentation). Although, Passarelli and Kolb do not directly and explicitly refer to Mezirow's transformative learning theory, they also recognise the importance of changes in frames of reference for learning to occur within experiential learning (2012). For them "all learning is relearning" that requires the examination and refinement of current beliefs and ideas, and for learning to occur "the resolution of conflicts between dialectically opposed modes of adaptation to the world" is required. Both experiential learning theory and transformative learning theory require the learners to take an active role in their learning; with reflection at the centre of it being an "active process of exploration and discovery which often leads to very unexpected outcomes" (Boud et al., 1985). For experiential learning this further includes engaging into actively questioning, discussing, solving problems through experimentations, and overall assuming responsibility of one's own learning (Kolb, 1984).

Experiential learning theory defines learning as a result of acquisition of new knowledge and interpretation and action as a result of this new knowledge, whereas transformative learning theory defines transformative learning as a change of frames of references. Peter Jarvis' definition brings the two together by defining learning as "the transformation of experience into *knowledge, skills and attitudes*, and [...which] occurs through a variety of processes". [added emphasis not in original] (2012, p. 8). Jarvis emphasises that learning can only occur within a social context, since the learner is a social construct, and hence "learning should be regarded as a social phenomenon as well as an individualistic one" (Jarvis, 2012, p. 15). Transformative learning theory also recognise that social interactions are fundamental for learning; and as Mezirow (1997) states "learning is a social process and discourse becomes central to making meaning." It is through these social interactions that learners' frame of references and their experiences can be transformed when learners' take responsibility and actively engage with their learning.

That learning is a social process was advocated by Lev Vygotsky. Vygotsky's learning theory proposes that through social interactions with more experienced and knowledgeable others, learners can expand their knowledge, problem-solving skills and performance. Central to this theory is the concept of the Zone of Proximal Development[3]. Within this zone are the tasks and knowledge that a learner can achieve with the support and guidance of a more experienced and capable person. The zone is considered a dynamic structure that is progressing together with the learner (Eun, 2019), and it is the learner that has to engage in active learning and take advantage of the collaboration to realise the performance beyond their immediate capabilities (Levykh, 2008). Outside of the Zone of Proximal Development are the tasks that are beyond the learner's reach even with support. It is only after mediation, through discourse, that the learner can internalise these new functions and be able to perform them independently. For instance, for transformative learning to occur the ability to critically reflect is essential. However, if the ability to critically reflect is absent, which may well be the case in educational settings that are traditionally more didactic and teacher-centred, the learner will rely on an authority to provide guidance of how to critically reflect and how to reach the best judgement through discourse. It is therefore essential that for transformative learning to occur, an initial level of guidance and instruction is required for the learners to become competent in critical reflection of theirs and others' views before they would be able to engage in critical reflection independently.

Lave and Wenger also advocate for a social learning theory, one that is situated in an authentic context environment (Lave & Wenger, 1991). Central to that is a community of practice that is defined as a group "of people who share a concern or a passion for something they do and learn how to do it better as they interact regularly" (Wenger-Trayner & Wenger-Trayner, 2015)[4]. A key premise of the community's formation, and hence level of success, is the variable level of experiences that the members bring as well as their motivation to engage with the community. An individual will join a community of practice as a novice in the periphery. The term 'legitimate peripheral participation' is used to emphasise the importance of active participation and engagement within the community that leads to learning while someone is still a novice but not just an observer (Lave & Wenger, 2001). The novice will be able to become a full or core participant of the specific community of practice through interactions with old-timers (Fuller et al., 2005). However, there is not a single trajectory for this to be achieved and not everyone will aspire to become a full participant (Handley et al., 2006). Independent of the trajectory or the aspirations of the individuals, within a community of practice the individual's identity has the potential to be constructed through changing forms of participation (Handley et al., 2006). Changing the individual's form of participation could further lead to the change of their frames of references and worldview as their position in the community is also altered. This further demonstrates how transformative learning experiences could be a direct result of active engagement and participation within a community that leads to the formation of new identities and sense of belonging.

By exploring the aforementioned learning theories, it becomes evident that learning is a social process that refers not only to the acquisition of new knowledge, skills and attributes, but also to the interpretation and assimilation of those by the learner. Learning can be transformative, by leading to the transformation of one's own self-conception and world perception as a result of critical reflections of discourse upon social interactions. A fundamental premise for transformative learning to occur is the active engagement and participation in those social interactions. However, on their own, active engagement and participation, and by extent active learning, will not necessarily lead to transformation if the newly acquired and interpreted knowledge, skills and attributes, can be assimilated within the pre-existing frames of references of the learner. To that end, we could divide active learning to informative and transformative active learning. With informative active learning, active participation and engagement results to the individual acquiring new knowledge, skills and attributes that are assimilated within the existing frames of reference. On the contrary, in transformative active learning, the active

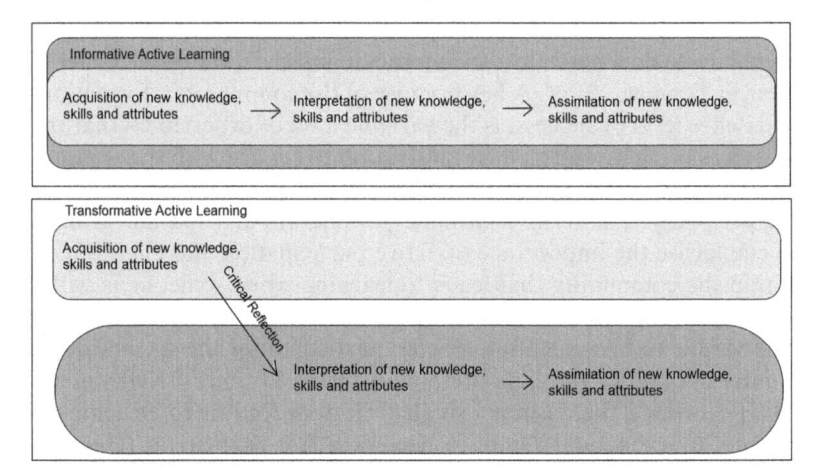

Figure 4.1 Informative and transformative active learning are an extension of the notions of informative and transformative learning (Engeström, 2001).

participation and engagement leads to the acquisition and interpretation of new knowledge, skills and attributes that lead to the transformation of the individual's frames of references as a result of critical reflection, before those newly acquired knowledge, skills and attributes, can be assimilated (Figure 4.1). In the next section of the chapter, I will bring the above observations together to define a framework of transformative active learning and the role that learning facilitators may play in creating the right learning environment to enable transformative learning.

The top panel shows the process of informative active learning. In informative active learning, the learner is actively engaged and participating within a social space, however all the steps of learning take place within the existing frame of reference (light grey). The assimilation of the new knowledge, skills and attributes may expand the fund of knowledge, skills and attributes within the existing frame of reference (dark grey) but will not transform the existing frame of reference. The lower panel shows the process of transformative active learning. Here the acquisition of new knowledge, skills and attributes within an active learning environment is followed by critical reflection that has the potential to change the existing frame of reference (light grey) to a new frame of reference (dark grey) before the new knowledge, skills and attributes can be assimilated. Although depicted as a linear process for ease, learning is a continuous, cyclical process where these steps can be repeated innumerable times.

A framework for transformative active learning

Through a theoretical exploration of a selection of learning theories, we were able to see that transformation could be achieved through active participation in critical reflective discourse within a group of people, of variable levels of knowledge and expertise and diverse experiences. Whereas Mezirow's transformative learning theory emphasises the importance of equality amongst learners', we can see that other social learning theories are strongly dependent on power dynamics that may result in empowering or disempowering experiences (Lave & Wenger, 1991). If we were to utilise transformative active learning within an HE setting, educators would need to carefully consider and address the power dynamics within the learning environment to ensure that transformative learning is a result of critical self-reflection, rather than imposed by an authority. As Mezirow states "The educator functions as a facilitator and provocateur rather than as an authority on subject matter" (Mezirow, 1997). Therefore, one of the key roles of the educator is the adaptation and maintenance of the learning environment to create the conditions for transformative learning experiences. The two required conditions for transformative learning in relation to the learning environment are tightly linked with the social aspect of transformative learning and those are:

1 the presence of a diverse group, comprised by learners, educators and others, with varying frames of references to allow for exposure to different worldviews and epistemologies, and
2 the careful consideration of the power dynamics within the above group and how those impact the discourse and interactions amongst participants.

Setting the appropriate learning environment is fundamental to enable the active engagement of the learner. But what constitutes active engagement and what are the pre-requisites for it to occur?

First and foremost, the learner needs to value their own past experiences and engage in critical self-reflection in order to understand and challenge their own current frames of reference. Educators can create the right environment and provide the right opportunities for self-reflection. However, they also need to be aware of the past experiences of their learners as well as of the current epistemological challenges that the learners face. To that end, if required, the educators will need to support the development of self and critical reflection skills. Secondly, the learner needs to be open to different views and frames of reference and actively engage in communicative discourse. Once again, the educators can create the appropriate learning environment that will foster opportunities for open communicative discourse and provide the essential support for the development of relevant skills for participation in discourse. Finally, the learner needs to critically reflect on their own and of others' views post discourse, which could potentially result in reframing their frames of references.

In summary, we can clearly see the central role of active learning within transformative learning experiences. As it is well known, in active learning, the learner takes ownership and moves from a passive learner that acts as a listener to an engaged learner (Bonwell & Eison, 1991) that is also actively reflecting and partakes in communicative discourse. Scaffolding is essential to develop those skills and hence educators will require to initially provide guidance and support until the learner is ready and confident to engage in transformative learning experiences.

Conclusion

This chapter aimed to make an explicit connection between transformative learning experiences and active learning and weave the two together, for creating a framework of transformative active learning, to be distinguished from informative active learning. Informative active learning allows the learner to gain further knowledge, skills and attributes that fit within their current frames of reference. Transformative active learning, on the contrary, allows the learners to change and transform their self-conception and world-perception through interactions and communicative discourse with others. For transformative learning to occur the learners need to master a set of skills that would allow participation in communicative discourse and critical reflection. The role of the educator, to that end, would be to support the learners to develop those skills and create the appropriate learning environments that lend themselves to transformative learning experiences. If we were to summarise a transformative learning experience it would look like this: The learners are supported to develop critical reflection skills, through which they are able to value their past experiences and understand and challenge their current frames of references. The educator brings together a group of people (learners and non-learners) with varying and diverse frames of reference and enables communicative discourse while being appreciative of the learning challenges that each of the learners faces at any given time. The learners are openly and freely engaging in communicative discourse, which is followed by critical reflection of their own and others' frames of references, with the potential to transform their frames of references. Intentionally embedding transformative active learning in HE may come with its challenges as it would require retraining the educators to be able to create the appropriate learning environments and utilise the most successful active learning strategies relevant to their disciplines. However, by intentionally incorporating transformative active learning within HE settings, students would be better prepared to meet the demands of a constantly transforming world and able to appreciate the importance of its diversity.

Acknowledgements

The author would like to thank Dr Babrak Ibrahimy for his support with the philosophical concepts that underpin several of the learning theories used in this chapter and for his constructive review of drafts.

Notes

1 Frame of reference according to Mezirow is a "mind-set or worldview of orienting assumptions and expectations involving values, beliefs, and concepts" (Dirkx et al., 2006).
2 "Free from coercion, distorting self-deception or immobilizing anxiety" (Mezirow, 2006, p. 2).
3 The Zone of Proximal Development is defined as "the distance between the actual development level as determined by independent problem solving and the level of potential development as determined through problem solving under adult guidance or in collaboration with more capable peers' (Vygotsky, 1978).
4 Later Wenger-Trayner and Wenger-Trayner adapted the concept to include landscapes of practice (2014), and although this is a very important aspect of how learning can take place and be influenced by a wide range of communities that an individual may be a member of, it goes beyond the scope of this chapter and therefore not addressed.

References

Abd Rahman, N. F., Mohd Yusof, K., Phang, F. A., Azizan, M. T., Mohd Addi, M., Sadikin, A. N., Tengku Malim Busu, T. N. Z., & Nawi, N. D. (2020). Developing rigor with critical discourse analysis to examine educators? transition toward active learning. *Procedia Computer Science, 172,* 49–54. https://doi.org/10.1016/j.procs.2020.05.007

Bonwell, C. C., & Eison, J. A. (1991). *Active Learning: Creating Excitement in the Classroom. ASHE-ERIC Higher Education Report No 1.* The George Washington University, School of Education and Human Development.

Boud, D., Keogh, R., & Walker, D. (1985). *Reflection: Turning Experience into learning* (D. Boud, R. Keogh, & D. Walker, Eds.). Routledge Falmer.

Chauhan, S., Gupta, P., Palvia, S., & Jaiswal, M. (2021). Information technology transforming higher education: A meta-analytic review. *Journal of Information Technology Case and Application Research, 23*(1), 3–35. https://doi.org/10.1080/15228053.2020.1846480

Dirkx, J. M., Mezirow, J., & Cranton, P. (2006). Musings and reflections on the meaning, context, and process of transformative learning: A dialogue between John M. Dirkx and Jack Mezirow. *Journal of Transformative Education, 4*(2), 123–139. https://doi.org/10.1177/1541344606287503

Engeström, Y. (2001). Expansive Learning at Work: Toward an activity theoretical reconceptualization. *Journal of Education and Work, 14*(1), 133–156. https://doi.org/10.1080/13639080020028747

Eun, B. (2019). The zone of proximal development as an overarching concept: A framework for synthesizing Vygotsky's theories. *Educational Philosophy and Theory, 51*(1), 18–30. https://doi.org/10.1080/00131857.2017.1421941

Evans, C., Rees, G., Taylor, C., & Fox, S. (2021). A liberal higher education for all? The massification of higher education and its implications for graduates' participation in civil society. *Higher Education, 81*(3), 521–535. https://doi.org/10.1007/s10734-020-00554-x

Fuller, A., Hodkinson, H., Hodkinson, P., & Unwin, L. (2005). Learning as peripheral participation in communities of practice: A reassessment of key concepts in workplace learning. *British Educational Research Journal, 31*(1), 49–68. https://doi.org/10.1080/0141192052000310029

Gouthro, P. A. (2006). Reason, communicative learning, and civil society: The use of Habermasian theory in adult education. *The Journal of Educational Thought (JET)/Revue de la Pensée Éducative, 40*(1), 5–22.

Habermas, J. (1981). *The Theory of Communicative Action, Vol 1.*

Handley, K., Sturdy, A., Fincham, R., & Clark, T. (2006). Within and beyond communities of practice: Making sense of learning through participation, identity and practice*. *Journal of Management Studies, 43*(3), 641–653.

Jarvis, P. (2012). *Adult Learning in the Social Context.* Routledge.

Kegan, R. (2009). What "form" transforms?: A constructive-developmental approach to transformative learning. In K. Illeris (Ed.), *Contemporary Theories of Learning: Learning Theorists – In Their Own Words* (pp. 35–54). Routledge.

Kolb, D. A. (1984). *Experiential Learning: Experience as the Source Of Learning And Development.* http://www.learningfromexperience.com/images/uploads/process-of-experiential-learning.pdf!

Lave, J., & Wenger, E. (1991). Situated learning: Legitimate peripheral participation. In: *Cambridge University Press.* Cambridge University Press.

Lave, J., & Wenger, E. (2001). Legitimate peripheral participation in communities of practice. In: *Supporting Lifelong Learning* (1st ed.). Routledge.

Levykh, M. G. (2008). The affective establishment and maintenance of Vygotsky's Zone of Proximal Development. *Educational Theory, 58*, 83–101. https://doi.org/https://doi.org/10.1111/j.1741-5446.2007.00277.x

McGuire, S., & McGuire, S. (2015). *Teaching Students How to Learn: Strategies You Can Incorporate in Any Course to Improve Student Metacognition, Study Skills and Motivation*. Stylus Publishing LLC.

Mezirow, J. (1978). Perspective transformation. *Adult Education, 28*(2), 100–110. https://doi.org/https://doi.org/10.1177/074171367802800202

Mezirow, J. (1981). A critical theory of adult learning and education. *Adult Education, 32*(1), 3–24. https://doi.org/https://doi.org/10.1177/074171368103200101

Mezirow, J. (1997). Transformative learning: Theory to practice. *New Directions for Adult and Continuing Education, 74*, 5–12. https://doi.org/https://doi.org/10.1002/ace.7401

Mezirow, J. (2006). An overview on transformative learning. In: J. Crowther & P. Sutherland (Eds.), *Lifelong Learning: Concepts and Contexts* (pp. 24–38). Routledge.

Passarelli, A. M., & Kolb, D. A. (2012). Using experiential learning theory to promote student learning and development in progams of education abroad. In: K. Hemming Lou, M. R. Paige, & M. van de Berg (Eds.), *Student Learning Abroad: What Our Students Are Learning, What They're Not, and What We Can Do about It*. Stylus Publishing LLC. http://ebookcentral.proquest.com/lib/coventry/detail.action?

Raikou, N., & Karalis, T. (2016). Adult education and higher education-a focus on transformative learning in universities. *International Education and Research Journal, 2*. https://www.researchgate.net/publication/305903415

Vygotsky, L. (1978). *Mind in Society: The Development of Higher Psychological Processes*. Harvard University Press.

Watermeyer, R., & Tomlinson, M. (2022). Competitive accountability and the dispossession of academic identity: Haunted by an impact phantom. *Educational Philosophy and Theory, 54*(1), 92–103. https://doi.org/10.1080/00131857.2021.1880388

Wenger-Trayner, E., & Wenger-Trayner, B. (2014). Learning in a landscape of practice A framework. In: *Learning in Landscapes of Practice Boundaries, Identity, and Knowledgeability in Practice-based Learning* (1st ed.). Routledge.

Wenger-Trayner, E., & Wenger-Trayner, B. (2015). *Communities of Practice a Brief Introduction*. https://wenger-trayner.com/introduction-to-communities-of-practice/

Wong, B., Chiu, Y. L. T., Copsey-Blake, M., & Nikolopoulou, M. (2021). A mapping of graduate attributes: What can we expect from UK university students? *Higher Education Research and Development*. https://doi.org/10.1080/07294360.2021.1882405

World Economic Forum. (2016). The Future of Jobs Employment, Skills and Workforce Strategy for the Fourth Industrial Revolution.

World Economic Forum. (2020). *The Future of Jobs Report 2020*.

5 Active cognitive tasks – Synthesising frameworks for active learning online

Mary Jacob

Introduction

It has long been recognised that active learning can help students engage with learning tasks, promote deeper learning and foster higher order thinking (Bonwell & Eison, 1991; Chickering & Gamson, 1987). Evidence shows the result can be better retention of actual learning (Deslauriers et al., 2019).

The sudden move to online and socially distanced teaching in response to the pandemic brought additional challenges to everyone in HE, especially in regard to active learning. Staff asked: "How can we promote active learning when teaching online? How can we do group work or class discussion in a socially distanced classroom? How can we enable students to learn actively when in-person lectures are replaced by recordings? How can we make a discussion board activity meaningful and motivating?"

The challenges are not just technical but also linked to underlying pedagogical principles.

To help staff in the pivot to online teaching in the summer of 2020, I devised a training session on 'Active Learning and Online Engagement'. As the coordinator of the Postgraduate Certificate in Teaching in HE (PGCTHE) and part of the Learning and Teaching Enhancement Unit at Aberystwyth University, I am interested in active learning and lessons from cognitive science about how students learn, so I drew on that literature when designing the session.

I chose four frameworks to create an integrated model for active learning and online engagement. The model is now embedded in our PGCTHE and used to train teaching staff across the university, with over 340 members of staff trained since summer 2020.

Definitions of active learning

There are many definitions of active learning. One of the earliest is by Chickering and Gamson, who include active learning as one of their

DOI: 10.4324/9781003360032-6

seven principles of undergraduate education. They emphasise the application of knowledge to students' daily lives, saying that students

> must talk about what they are learning, write about it [...] make what they learn part of themselves.
> (Chickering & Gamson, 1987, p. 4)

Building on that foundation, Bonwell and Eison define active learning as instructional activities that 'involve students in doing things and thinking about what they are doing'. They note that active learning places less emphasis on transmission of information and more emphasis on skills, and also that students should be required to engage in activities where they explore their own attitudes and values (Bonwell & Eison, 1991, p. 2). The emphasis here is on having students carry out tasks through which they learn.

The early definitions of active learning are framed in terms that call for a change from established teaching methods. Chickering and Gamson say that:

> learning is not a spectator sport. Students do not learn much just by sitting in classes listening to teachers, memorizing prepackaged assignments, and spitting out answers.
> (1987, p. 4)

Bonwell and Eison concur, saying that active learning occurs when:

> students are involved in more than just listening.
> (1991, p. 2)

Working with these early definitions in conjunction with later research, I've come to consider active learning to be any activity where students carry out an Active Cognitive Task (ACT). As suggested by the name, an ACT has three essential elements:

1 **Task** – Student must carry out a task, not just absorb information or perform an operation by rote. It is not the content itself but what they do with it that matters.
2 **Cognitive** – The task must involve thinking, a cognitive engagement with new ideas. Both the early definitions and recent research in cognitive science emphasise thinking. Students drive new information into long-term memory so they can use it in a meaningful way. This is the constructive aspect of learning, where students create mental schemas by reinforcing connections between ideas.

Because this mental work can be hard, it is sometimes referred to as 'effortful learning' (Brown et al., 2014) or 'desirable difficulty' (Bjork, 1994).

3 **Active** – The task must be active, not passive, such that students take responsibility and ownership of the learning process. This requires building mutual trust and giving students agency.

Challenges of active learning online

For those accustomed to lecturing, it can be a challenge to use active learning, even more so when making a shift from in-person to online teaching. Staff who already use active learning in the classroom may also find it hard to retain active learning when moving online, and thus risk falling back on recording transmission-style lectures or using discussion boards in an unstructured way.

Without having a clearly defined ACT, students may not learn much from lecture recordings and may not even watch them. Discussion boards can be powerful learning tools, but if the ACT is not made explicit, students may not understand what type of post is required. Giving students a topic or reading and just asking them to 'discuss' often results in disengagement or posts with insufficient depth.

It isn't necessary to eliminate all lecturing as long as the lecture component serves as a primer for the ACT and not an end in itself. Depending on the institutional context, this may require a culture change.

Active learning can be incorporated by breaking up synchronous or asynchronous lectures with frequent interactions such as online quizzes or group discussions. Another option is to deliver a mini-lecture and then give students time to use the information to solve problems or complete a short writing task. In both cases, the ACT should be specified to students with the cognitive element clearly explained and the link between the ACT and other elements of the teaching made explicit.

In the Learning and Teaching Enhancement Unit, we recommend that staff start small so that any teaching intervention is manageable and sustainable. It can be hard for students to adjust if the teacher changes modes in the middle of a module, so we also recommend starting active learning as early as possible to help students set appropriate expectations.

Synthesising frameworks

To meet these challenges of active learning online, I selected four frameworks and synthesised them into a unified model for designing

ACTs. Although intended to support online learning, the model can also be applied to classroom-based teaching. The frameworks are:

- ABC Learning Design (ABC LD)
- Bloom's taxonomy
- ICAP framework
- Online Engagement Framework for Higher Education

When mapped against each other, these four frameworks offer a stimulating array of options for practical application of ACTs in both online and in-person teaching.

ABC learning design

ABC LD was developed at UCL and has been widely implemented globally. Young and Perović (2016) build their framework around Laurillard's types of learning (2012), which support the Active component of ACTs. Laurillard describes learning as an "active process" (2012, p. 61). The types are Acquisition, Inquiry (or Investigation), Discussion, Practice, Collaboration and Production.

The descriptions below are based on the ABC LD toolkit (Young and Perović, 2020):

- **Acquisition** – Absorb information transmitted by teachers, books, videos, etc.
- **Collaboration** – Work together with peers towards a goal.
- **Investigation** – Study or research independently, going beyond transmitted content.
- **Discussion** – Articulate and respond to ideas with peers or teaching staff.
- **Practice** – Develop a skill using feedback, adapting to the task goal.
- **Production** – Create something, consolidate what is learned.

ABC LD is not prescriptive but rather encourages staff to seek a balance across the six types that is suitable for their own teaching context. It can help teachers think of options other than standard default choices such as lecture. One ACT may include several types of learning.

Most of these types are active by their nature, but Laurillard notes that in Acquisition, the student may play:

> a relatively passive role while the teacher uses the transmission style of teaching.
>
> (2012, p. 105)

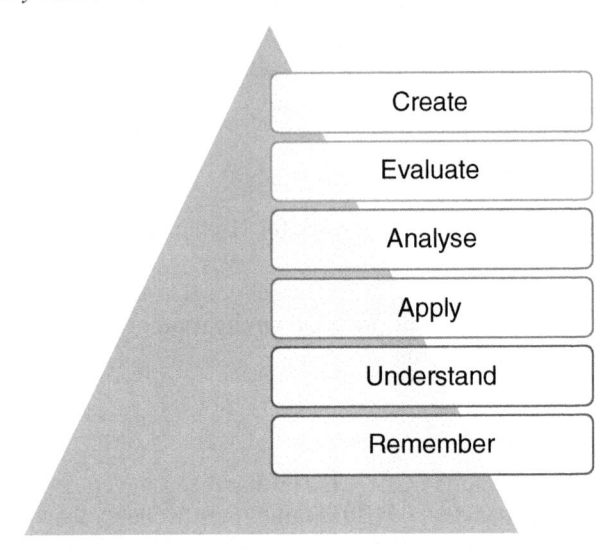

Figure 5.1 Bloom's taxonomy, revised version (Anderson and Krathwohl, 2001).

Acquisition can be made more active if students carry out an ACT while listening to a lecture or reading, for example, thinking of real-world examples for abstract concepts, linking new material to previously learned material, constructing definitions in their own words for key terms and so on. Students test their ideas in subsequent activities where they receive feedback such as blog posts or seminar discussion.

Bloom's taxonomy of educational objectives in the cognitive domain

Bloom's taxonomy is a familiar framework widely used in higher education. The higher orders of thinking within Bloom's taxonomy support the Cognitive component of ACTs.

Bloom's original version (1956) uses nouns for each level. Working downwards from the highest levels of thinking, Bloom describes them as: Evaluation, Synthesis, Analysis, Application, Comprehension and Knowledge (recall).

In their revised taxonomy, Anderson et al. (2001) rename 'Synthesis' as 'Create' and use active verbs rather than nouns. Here I use the revised version because the verbs can gracefully be used to design active tasks (Figure 5.1).

Bonwell and Eison make a direct link between active learning and the taxonomy (using Bloom's original version), stating that when active learning takes place:

> students are engaged in such higher-order thinking (analysis, synthesis, and evaluation).
>
> (1991, p. 2)

The levels are increasingly active as one moves up the pyramid. It is worth noting that the higher levels include levels below them, for example, a student must understand and remember ideas in order to apply them to a new situation or analyse a complex system.

Verbs in the top four levels are especially useful for constructing ACTs. While ABC LD provides multiple options for *how* students carry out a task, Bloom's taxonomy sheds light on *what* students do from a cognitive perspective.

Interactive-constructive-active-passive (ICAP) model

The ICAP model by Chi differentiates categories within active learning as 'active, constructive, and interactive in terms of observable overt activities and underlying learning processes' (2009, p. 73). Chi's framework is useful for designing the Task component of ACTs as well as taking the cognitive dimension into consideration.

- The **Active** category involves 'engaging activities' and attending to existing knowledge. This may require tasks such as selecting, paraphrasing, etc.
- The **Constructive** category requires 'self-construction activities' and individual creation. Typical tasks include producing output beyond what is given by the instructor, such as elaborating or predicting outcomes.
- The **Interactive** category requires 'guided-construction and co-construction activities' through instructional and joint dialogue. Tasks often involve giving and responding to feedback.

Chi contrasts these types of active learning with **Passive** learning in which there are no overt activities. Thus:

> if students were merely watching a video recording [...] without being able to explore or manipulate the environment, that would

be considered to be passive in that, at least overtly, the student is not doing anything.

(2009, p. 76)

Chi analyses the relative effectiveness of these categories, noting that '*interactive* activities are better than *constructive*, which are better than *active*, which are better than *passive*' (2009, p. 89).

Chi's framework can help staff evaluate and choose tasks that are more effective for learning.

Online engagement framework for higher education

Redmond's Online Engagement Framework for Higher Education framework (2018) is designed for online teaching but also applicable to classroom-based teaching. It places the Cognitive dimension of learning into a broader context, extending beyond the cognitive domain with five interrelated elements. Redmond notes that these elements are not hierarchical but rather offer 'a tool to unpack the dynamic nature of online engagement' (2009, p. 190). The summaries below are drawn from the full framework:

- **Cognitive engagement** – The 'active process of learning', what happens inside the students' minds, engagement with the subject material.
- **Behavioural engagement** – 'Conduct, participation', i.e. observable external behaviours.
- **Social engagement** – 'Building community, creating a sense of belonging', which may or may not be directly related to the subject material.
- **Collaborative engagement** – 'Learning with peers, developing professional networks'. This element is explicitly connected to the subject material and is more effective when supported by social engagement as well.
- **Emotional engagement** – 'Emotional reaction to learning, attitude, enthusiasm, interest, anxiety or enjoyment in the learning process', which includes motivation, confidence, barriers to learning, etc.

Cross-mapping active learning frameworks

In exploring the literature from pedagogy and cognitive science, I am struck by the confluence of these frameworks. Although the finer

Active cognitive tasks 53

Table 5.1 Cross-mapping Three Active Learning Frameworks

ABC LD	ICAP	Bloom's Taxonomy
Acquisition	Passive	Remember
Collaboration	Interactive	Depends on task
Investigation	Constructive	Evaluate
Discussion	Interactive	Understand
Practice	Active	Apply
Production	Constructive	Create

details of how an activity is implemented can make a difference as to which category it falls into, there are many natural affinities across the frameworks (Table 5.1).

Acquisition primarily requires Remembering and has potential to be passive, but it can be active providing that the instructor has given students an ACT to carry out. This can be as simple as providing guidance for taking notes. In an online environment where recorded lectures are used, it is crucial to ensure that students know what task they are meant to do while watching recordings. The same principle applies to ACTs for reading texts.

Collaboration is a natural fit with Interactive learning. The specific nature of the cognitive task that students undertake during their collaboration determines which level of Bloom's taxonomy is most applicable. In most group work for university courses, students make something such as a poster, a robot, a business plan, etc. This is likely to require higher order thinking such as Create.

Investigation (also called Inquiry) is Constructive by its nature and likely to require Evaluation.

Discussion requires Interactivity. The nature of the task determines which level on Bloom's taxonomy is most appropriate. At a minimum, student discussion involves clarifying Understanding, but it can require higher order thinking if, for example, the task includes evaluating evidence or constructing persuasive arguments.

Practice can be simple or complex, depending on the ACT. When carried out on a basic level such as practicing a laboratory technique or solving a mathematical problem, it is likely to be Active or Constructive and require that the student Applies prior knowledge to a new situation.

Production aligns with the Constructive element of ICAP and Create on Bloom's taxonomy.

Table 5.2 Mapping ABC LD with Online Engagement

	Cognitive	Behavioural	Collaborative	Social	Emotional
Acquisition	X	Maybe	No	No	Precondition
Collaboration	X	X	X	X	Precondition
Investigation	X	X	Maybe	Maybe	Precondition
Discussion	X	X	X	X	Precondition
Practice	X	X	Maybe	Maybe	Precondition
Production	X	X	Maybe	Maybe	Precondition

Cross-mapping active learning with online engagement

Mapping the ABC LD types of learning against Redmond's framework offers a revealing pattern (Table 5.2).

All of the ABC LD types of learning require Cognitive engagement and most require Behavioural engagement. Behavioural engagement is more visible than Cognitive engagement and easier to gauge, however, so teaching staff may need to pay more deliberate attention to fostering Cognitive engagement.

For example, having students make one discussion board post and respond to three others requires Behavioural engagement. Teachers can foster Cognitive engagement by making the ACT more explicit, such as requiring students to offer one real-world example of the principle being taught and evaluate three examples from classmates based on how closely the examples express the principle.

Collaborative and Social engagement *may* come into play with Investigation, Practice and Production, but only if students work in groups or pairs. Both the ICAP model and Redmond's framework encourage teaching staff to have students work together to learn. In classroom-based learning, collaborative engagement is easier to foster and social engagement often arises without the teacher's intervention. Online learning, however, requires a more intentional approach to ensure that students have an opportunity to engage in these ways.

Emotional engagement pertains to motivation and other affective elements that serve as a precondition to learning. Without emotional engagement, students are unlikely to carry out any type of task. In a classroom, teachers can promote emotional engagement by observing and responding to non-verbal behaviour. In an online environment, however, teachers may need a more pro-active approach to understand how well their students are engaging emotionally. Giving students agency, as in the Active element of an ACT, can go a long way towards fostering emotional engagement.

The ACT model provides an integrated approach to using the four frameworks. I use the active learning approaches from the model when I facilitate workshops. For example, first I have participants watch a recording and think about how they might apply the principles to their own teaching. In the live online session, they write their ideas into a shared document. This allows more participants to contribute than speaking alone would. The document then forms the basis for a whole-group discussion where we elaborate and develop the ideas collaboratively.

The ACT model can help teaching staff think beyond standard default choices for online teaching that may consist of diminished versions of face-to-face teaching methods. For example, a teacher who uses active learning techniques to incorporate questioning and discussions into a classroom-based lecture may struggle to find an online equivalent that goes beyond a transmission-style lecture recording. The key to making lecture recordings effective is to give students an active cognitive task associated with the recordings. The ACT model thus encourages staff to think in concrete terms to find new options and foster active learning online.

References

Anderson, L. W., Krathwohl, D. R., Airasian, P. W., Cruikshank, K. A., Mayer, R. E., Pintrich, P. R., Raths, J. D., and Bloom, B. S. (2001) *A taxonomy for learning, teaching, and assessing: A revision of Bloom's Taxonomy of educational objectives*, New York: Addison-Wesley.

Bjork, R. A. (1994) 'Memory and metamemory considerations in the training of human beings,' *Metacognition: Knowing about knowing*, edited by Janet Metcalfe and Arthur Shimamura, Cambridge, MA: MIT Press, pp. 185–205.

Bloom, B. S. (1956) *Taxonomy of educational objectives: the classification of educational goals*, New York: David McKay Co.

Bonwell, C. C. and Eison, J. A. (1991) *Active learning: Creating excitement in the classroom*, Washington, DC: School of Education and Human Development, George Washington University.

Brown, P. C., Roediger, H. L., and McDaniel, M. A. (2014) *Make it stick: the science of successful learning*, Cambridge, MA: The Belknap Press of Harvard University Press.

Chi, M. T. H. (2009) 'Active-constructive-interactive: a conceptual framework for differentiating learning activities,' *Topics in Cognitive Science*, 1(1), pp. 73–105.

Chickering, A. W. and Gamson, Z. F. (1987). 'Seven principles for good practice in undergraduate education,' *AAHE Bulletin*, pp. 3–7.

Deslauriers, L., McCarty, L. S., Callaghan, K., Kestin, G., McCarty, L. S., and Miller, K. (2019) 'Measuring actual learning versus feeling of learning in response to being actively engaged in the classroom,' *Proceedings of the National Academy of Sciences of the United States of America*, 116(39), pp. 19251–19257.

Laurillard, D. (2012) *Teaching as a design science: Building pedagogical patterns for learning and technology*, New York, NY: Routledge.

Redmond, P., Heffernan, A., Abawi, L., Brown, A., and Henderson, R. (2018), 'An online engagement framework for higher education,' *Online Learning*, 22(1), pp. 183–204.

Young, C and Perović, N (2016), 'Rapid and Creative Course Design: As Easy as ABC?,' *Procedia – Social and Behavioral Sciences*, 228, pp. 390–395.

Young, C. and Perović, N. (2020) *ABC Learning Design Toolkit*.

6 Prospects for coactive learning
Sam Elkington

Introduction

Since March 2020, hybrid education has moved to become almost the de-facto norm for a global higher education sector. The swift proliferation of digital learning technologies accompanying this movement has meant that educators have had to adapt to the demands of changing patterns of work and student learning, with the enactment of academic practice occurring across a multitude of sprawling, inter-connected, digital, and physical environments. While most learning experiences have been digitised in the form of online classes or other formats in which the learning experience is predominantly virtual, other learning experiences have involved a return to physical learning spaces that have also involved combinations of synchronous and asynchronous online learning for presentation, simulation, access to data, and virtual forms of interaction and collaboration. The 'hybridisation' of the physical and virtual or digital learning space is a critical aspect of the emerging requirements of 'flexible learning environments' at every scale, blurring the boundaries between distinct contexts of learning and their activities, and the often surprising, interleaved experiences they can engender.

In response, this chapter explores how taking a broader person-environment system view when working with the affordances of such hybrid spaces can open up new ways of placing and harnessing learning that is inherently *'co-active'* in spaces that are more highly connected, permeable, and networked (physically and digitally) to provide flexible and adaptable learning environments.

The onset of hybrid learning and challenges to space and pedagogy

Hybrid learning spaces open up opportunities and pose challenges to educators. Such spaces have the potential to promote significant

DOI: 10.4324/9781003360032-7

learning, allowing a more expansive suite of integrated pedagogic arrangements and assemblages that span the digital and physical tools and spaces mediating students' interactions with the wider learning environment (Saichaie, 2020). From this broader 'person-environment' perspective, navigating such hybridity is not solely a technical or technological issue; a hybrid pedagogy fundamentally rethinks the places in which learning occurs, as students and educators are connected and interact through a network of physical and technologically mediated encounters, each playing a coactive role in constructing knowledge and positioning practices necessary for meaningful learning.

Higher education systems are beginning to recognise the potential of hybrid learning spaces for fostering active learning through the increasing use of pedagogical hybrid models and approaches centred on the learning needs of students (Goodyear, 2020). Active learning involves a pedagogical shift from instructor-focused teaching to a contextualised, student-focused, process of constructing knowledge and experiences of learning that are rarely symmetrical. Such prospective asymmetry is particularly problematic when we talk about flexible, distance, and/or blended learning. Indeed, what makes sense to the educator in one context (i.e., a classroom-based discussion) may well prove unrecognisable and thus inaccessible to different learners from the same cohort depending on their circumstances and mode of study (i.e., students engaging with a classroom-based discussion remotely). It follows that within hybrid contexts, influence over the construction of action and meaning is distributed throughout the coacting elements of the person-environment system.

This introduces some key ideas and thinking about flexibility, the situated nature of learning, and the relations between the act of learning and situations in which students have greater control over the learning process (Goodyear, 2020; Saichaie, 2020). Here, following Ellis and Goodyear (2016), the concept of 'learning place' is used deliberately as a way of indicating something more specific and concrete (in experiential terms) than space, something that is imbued with meaning and value through the coactive participation of student and educator in shaping both its form and function. This focus on learning places connects to a growing acknowledgment of the importance of arrangements of physical and virtual environments in influencing how and what people learn (Goodyear, 2020).

Change and innovation in educational technology has allowed a shift in expectations, practices, and discourse around how learning is situated in space and time with these learning places affording the reconfiguration of different digital tools, activities, and interactions to make it possible to work with knowledge in new and engaging ways. Though their approaches to learning and levels of digital literacy may vary, students are using the affordances of different digital tools and platforms to discover and construct knowledge that is meaningful to their learning needs and, as a result, are increasingly coming to expect to be provided with wider, sometimes ubiquitous access to educational resources. For Goodyear (Goodyear, Ellis, and Marmot, 2018; Goodyear, 2020), the concept of affordances is a relational construct where the qualities of a tool or task and the capabilities of a person come together to describe what the tool or task offers the person for their learning.

This points to the impact of the learner's context when determining the affordance of certain combinations of tools and spaces for learning. From this person-environment system perspective, learning is coactively produced, and learners and teachers are always entangled with different places, tools, and resources during the practice of teaching and learning (Carvalho and Yeoman, 2018).

Putting coactive learning strategies in place

Variations of active learning include collaborative, cooperative, and project-based learning. All three approaches encourage students to be involved actively in the learning process, however, each prioritises slightly different factors in learning.

In collaborative work active learning occurs when students are encouraged to explore new solutions based on existing knowledge sharing ideas with peers and immersive participation in the process of learning. Collaborative learning typically refers to students working together in small groups towards a shared goal with the interaction between group members the key feature.

Cooperative learning refers to group-based work with a common end goal where the assessment is individual. Although assessment is usually individual in this form of learning, cooperation between group members is encouraged to promote peer learning and support.

Project-based learning can be cooperative and collaborative but is also often individual involving research and investigation activities in response to set (or negotiated) problems and tasks. Through an emphasis on inquiry learning, problem-based approaches make use of resources that provide searchable access to a range of information, data, knowledge, and ideas, both conventional and digital. Crucially, students are in control of the sequence of information and can follow their own line or inquiry, making them active participants, and giving them a greater sense of ownership of their learning.

A present challenge for educators is to understand how the shifting material, digital, and hybrid assemblages of places, tools, and resources can be effectively configured to promote active, connected, learning in manageable and sustainable ways. Set out below are three pedagogic strategies designed to animate collaborative, cooperative, and project-based learning in blended educational environments. Each strategy offers a practical illustration of how digital learning tools and techniques can be combined and configured to provide places for *coactive learning* and activities that generate real-time, actionable insights into individual and social learning processes, providing a timely look into how active learning is becoming more nuanced through proliferation of hybrid learning spaces.

Fostering meaningful collaboration

In collaborative learning the focus is the social and cultural description of how groups of students construct a shared outcome, negotiated through dialogue and debate (Laurillard, 2013). Digital tools and resources can be used to support productive communication between participants and the construction and exposition of different representations and positions by leveraging their unique affordances, rather than just replicating what can be done face-to-face. The issue is how best to support students in managing the discussion-solution process to get the intended value from the collaborative act. One possible hybrid configuration to encourage meaningful collaboration in a seminar setting is to set up a single shared 'class' form to structure and capture this process using collaborative digital tools such as Microsoft Forms or OneNote and asking students to work in pairs or small groups to discuss and record their 'shared' responses to a challenging task directly on the shared form.

Collaborative notetaking tools are a useful means of encouraging student engagement around shared activities supporting opportunities for peer modelling, where students can learn from how the other works and communicates (Cope and Kalantzis, 2017). Being motivated to practice with one another, to spend time on generating, articulating, and critiquing their ideas and points of view, is more likely to happen as part of a supportive shared environment than in individual learning. The ability to offload or share thoughts and ideas to an artifact co-produced in the learning place is also a strong influence on what is cognitively possible for students, as well as a skill in itself to be mastered.

To ensure students spend their time productively, it can be useful for educators to design scripted (or scaffolded) guidance that not only clarifies the nature of the task, along with information about specialised task resources available to students which may be physical and/or digital – i.e., a location such as a lab, performance space, or digital simulation. It should also be designed with a view to rehearsing students in the ways of thinking and practicing in their field. Keeping the shared form 'live' post-session can encourage continued student engagement with key topics through asynchronous contributions in response to 'follow-up' questioning and peer engagement focused on individual and/or shared key learning. It can also be useful to encourage students to get into the habit of recording any questions they might have regarding the task or topics directly on the shared form. This allows the educator to respond in a timely fashion to any general issues or misunderstandings at a group level and creates a record of student input and progress that can be revisited at a later date to help inform subsequent active learning designs. In this way digital and physical tools at once mediate and shape students' interactions in and with learning space(s) (Carvalho and Yeoman, 2018), imbuing them with meaning and value through the co-production of social processes geared at enhancing their dispositions as learners to participate and engage knowledgeably as part of a broader person-environment system.

Encouraging rich interactions and discussion

Conventional forms of learning through discussion vary principally in the size of the group being taught, and the degree to which the teacher leads. The classic discussion group format typically involves teacher-led discussion of a specific topic, problem, or case, where students are encouraged to develop their solutions or opinions through interaction with each other, guided by the teacher. With the expansion of communicative media afforded by today's digital technologies such interactions can now be designed to occur either asynchronously or synchronously. Though established digital discussion tools such as online discussion boards substitute oral discussions in the traditional classroom assemblage for digital text-based dialogues, to support various forms of conversational interaction online.

Pedagogically, this shift between asynchronous and synchronous teaching is important because it recalibrates the way both teachers and students spend their time in discussion (Laurillard, 2012). Encouraging learning-centred discussion helps students develop critical thinking and autonomy in learning by engaging in spontaneous expression of their ideas, and to clarify and deepen their understanding through dialogue and debate (Cope and Kalantzis, 2017). But with many students demanding greater flexibility in order to fit their studies around other aspects of their lives, the boundaries between physical and virtual learning encounters are becoming less clear and more permeable. Digital learning tools and technologies make a different kind of contribution here, providing not just access to resources 'for' discussion, but more importantly, open pedagogical layouts and assemblages of tools and places that afford the reconfiguration and redistribution of learning 'through' discussion and meaningful interactions across space and time.

Making use of live polling or quiz tools can provide students with regular opportunities to gauge their understanding of topics and concepts and offers a shared platform from which to discuss and explore course material. Using tools like Socrative during face-to-face (and online) sessions can boost engagement by quickly checking student knowledge, promoting in class participation and interaction, and providing timely (formative) feedback. Live polling and quizzes are an effective means of gathering actionable data regarding student learning, with tools such as Socrative offering a range of question formats (i.e., MCQs, single-right answer, short-answer). It is important educators give careful thought to the kinds of information they wish to capture and whether it is timely, relevant, and useful given the learning objectives. Framing student interaction and discussion around key ideas using quick question-style exercises at the beginning and/or the end of a session affords an inclusive way of involving students, gathering insight into their progress, and identifying gaps in knowledge. This instant feedback can be used to inform the content and flow of sessions by addressing gaps in real time, through dialogue and targeted work.

Using digital tools like Microsoft Forms, with its ability to add branching questions and sections, to ask more complex questions in the form of a digital dialogue sheet can provide another means of generating structured interaction and discussion around key ideas. The digital dialogue sheet might be completed either prior to or at the beginning of a session, providing the basis for more focused discussion around emergent themes and ideas. Several forms can be generated to enable smaller groups of students to explore different themes or related topics simultaneously before coming together to share and consider key insights. An advantage of using a tool like Microsoft Forms for devising such digital dialogue sheets is that a visual summary of responses is provided, and all data can be saved and exported to be used to inform subsequent interactions. Such strategies permit and promote the redistribution of student learning in space and time, the interleaving of formal and informal social structures and processes offering ways of working with learning spaces such that they can be co-produced for a common good; helping staff and students shape shared places for meaningful learning.

Learning through worked examples of scenarios or problem tasks

Learning through worked examples of a scenario or problem is an effective way to learn how to carry out a task or form of inquiry or solve a problem in an area where the learner has little prior knowledge. Having students actively engage with worked examples can illustrate key principles or patterns of information which help them to identify relevant information to map to similar or different problems. Prior to releasing worked examples, it can be useful to first provide students with 2 to 3 partial scenarios capturing actual or hypothetical real-life illustrations of a topic or problem, asking them to choose a scenario to investigate and report how they would respond. This can be easily facilitated by sharing each scenario with students as a digital resource via a VLE or Microsoft Teams and tasking them to document their thoughts on a discussion board or online chat using their own devises. Student contributions can then form the basis for a whole-class discussion of each scenario in turn after which the teacher unveils the full detail of each worked example, including the actual solutions deployed and key steps taken to generate and achieve each solution.

Such a scaffolded approach sets up an important 'process-orientation' and a focus on developing a working appreciation of the underlying structural aspects of the worked examples provided. To encourage extended interaction and discussion another strategy is to set up each scenario as a separate 'Breakout Room' (through the channel feature available on MS Teams) and ask students to document their thoughts for all scenarios/problems within a set period of time. Responses can then be reviewed, in turn, with the class. Backchannelling student interaction using online text chat during face-to-face sessions provides a forum for supplemental discussions among students around scenarios or problem tasks. This also serves a broader universal design purpose by providing a written alternative to spoken discussions which some students can find challenging and uncomfortable. Making use of collaborative tools like Microsoft OneNote or Padlet to facilitate extended cooperative group work on a scenario or problem task can also enable groups of students to work across multiple spaces and time frames to produce a shared response to a scenario or problem by collating and co-editing content that can be easily shared with the wider class. Educators can then review all contributions and highlight a selection of responses to share with the full group along with comments reflecting on and synthesising student idea as formative feedback to the group.

This combination of activities is intended to merge classroom sessions with online features to promote active, self-directed experiences for learners, which is, in turn, revealed as 'situated' practice (Kemmis et al., 2014) with teachers and learners co-configuring a complex of distributed learning spaces that shape episodes of hybrid learning.

Conclusion

The inherent complexity of emerging hybrid teaching and learning is apparent in each of these strategies for coactive learning as students and teachers choose, or are increasingly required, to work in synchronous or asynchronous teaching and learning spaces that are accessed from a multitude of physical and virtual places (e.g., on-campus classroom or computer laboratory, home, or other workplaces). Set against the backdrop of changing patterns of 'distributed' learning and working, combined with the proliferation of digital learning tools and technologies in HE, prospects for coactive learning need to be considered less in terms of singular learning spaces and much more in terms of a person-environment system for networked, inter-connected hybrid, physical, and virtual learning experiences in which digital tools, resources and places are an integral aspect of pedagogic design. Such a view implies a widening and loosening of the boundaries of conventional learning spaces to provide greater potential flexibility in how, where, and when learning happens. However, inviting greater flexibility is accompanied by dangers of fragmentation, as learners become spread across multiple spaces, devices, and media, interacting with different groups of people at different times. A challenge for educators when taking a broader person-environment system view is to utilise material, digital and hybrid tools, and resources to devise pedagogic patterns and assemblages that promote coactive learning to help students (re)connect what they are learning – ideas to thinking, principles to problems, theory to practice, learning to life.

References

Carvalho, L., & Yeoman, P. (2018). Framing learning entanglement in innovative learning spaces: Connecting theory, design and practice. *British Educational Research Journal, 44*(6), 1120–1137.

Cope, B., & Kalantzis, M. (Eds.). (2017). *E-learning ecologies: Principles for new learning and assessment.* London: Taylor & Francis.

Ellis, R. A., & Goodyear, P. (2016). Models of learning space: integrating research on space, place and learning in higher education. *Review of Education, 4*(2), 149–191.

Goodyear, P. (2020). Design and co-configuration for hybrid learning: Theorising the practices of learning space design. *British Journal of Educational Technology, 51*(4), 1045–1060.

Goodyear, P., Ellis, R. A., & Marmot, A. (2018). Learning spaces research: Framing actionable knowledge. In *Spaces of teaching and learning* (pp. 221–238). Singapore: Springer.

Kemmis, S., Wilkinson, J., Edwards-Groves, C., Hardy, I., Grootenboer, P., & Bristol, L. (2014). *Changing practices, changing education.* Singapore, Singapore: Springer.

Laurillard, D. (2013). *Teaching as a design science: Building pedagogical patterns for learning and technology.* London: Routledge.

Saichaie, K. (2020). Blended, flipped, and hybrid learning: definitions, developments, and directions. *New Directions for Teaching and Learning, 2020*(164), 95–104.

7 From theory to practice – Active learning in the flow of clinical work

Nick Leney and Helen Winter

The International Consortium for Personalized Medicine (Vicente, et al. 2020) forecasts an ever-escalating role for processed data in clinical care and a health delivery-associated transformation.

Personalized Medicine (PM) (Nimmesgern, et al. 2017) follows traditional evidence-based practices (EBM) (Sackett, et al. 1996) and maintains the cardinality of primary patient data in diagnosis and treatment. The canonical wisdom of placing the patient at the centre of practice and famously extolled by Sir William Osler (Cranston 2017) is confirmed and now possible through a vastly enlarged evidence base.

> **PERSONALIZED MEDICINE (PM)**
>
> 'Personalized medicine refers to a medical model using characterization of individuals' phenotypes and genotypes (e.g. molecular profiling, medical imaging and lifestyle data) for tailoring the right therapeutic strategy for the right person at the right time'

> The good physician treats the disease; the great physician treats the patient who has the disease.
>
> Osler p. 20, Cranston 2017

Invigorated by biotechnology and new data sources, PM requires extensive adjustments in healthcare provision, albeit the underlying methodology remains intact. Provider modifications include better strategic collaboration, agile care planning and an associated capacity to learn and assimilate best-practice from rising

> **EVIDENCE-BASED MEDICINE (EBM)**
>
> 'The conscientious and judicious use of current best evidence from clinical care research in the management of individual patients'

DOI: 10.4324/9781003360032-8

evidence. The transition in practice to PM faces significant logistical, cultural barriers and the delivery of training interventions to mitigate existing and emerging skills and practice gaps.

PM increasingly necessitates the clinical team to function as agile knowledge workers with vocational behaviours and beliefs evolving by experience and processing new information. By recognizing that future practice must rapidly evolve from current evidence-based treatment, one must accept that sustainable professionalism will not be completed or sustained without continuous learning.

This chapter explores how active learning (AL) may democratize and accelerate professional learning and presents practical applications of the methodology within the business as usual activities of clinical teams.

Learning at work is an outcome of diverse experiential activities, and in NHS, clinical teams commonly manifest in utilitarian and passive training interventions predicated upon defined priority areas. While effective in personal learning, AL is better when deployed across professional teams and supports clinicians to thrive as knowledge workers for the best interest of patients and clinicians and the delivery of excellence in up-to-date care.

> **ACTIVE LEARNING (AL)**
>
> 'Active learning engages students as leaders in the process of learning by activities and/or discussion, as opposed to passively listening to an expert'.

The need for active learning

Embedding active learning in the workplace is essential to learning at the scale required by contemporary teams operating as knowledge workers. Table 7.1 exemplifies typical active and passive tasks. Critical differences between approaches include the two-way communication of active learning and the egalitarian relationship between student and tutor in the active learning flow.

Learning patterns within NHS clinical teams are not unique to medicine and are evident in Lombardo & Eichinger's analysis of self-reported learning from nearly 200 executives (Lombardo & Eichinger 1996). The model that emerged from the collected data attributed just 10% of vocational education to off-the-job courses, 20% to interactions with peers, for example, mentoring, and the 70% majority, to experience gained in the act of work. Despite dispute and criticism from first publishing, not least for the convenient proportions of the model, the emphasis placed on professional learning achieved during work was timely and needed.

Table 7.1 Examples of Active v Passive Learning

Active Learning	Passive Learning
Seeking the individual opinion/ recommendation/ feedback to matters arising, e.g. wellbeing of a new patient; implementation of new protocols or therapies.	Presenting a case report to a colleague during a Team meeting.
Providing opportunity for colleague questions during a case review.	Organizing an expert speaker to present via webinar on their groundbreaking research.
The self-monitoring of professional development and professional learning needs.	Publishing on the intranet a PowerPoint library of reference cases.
The use of whole team quality circles to identified Team weaknesses and solutions.	Circulating MDT notes to the entire medical care team.
Establishing a regional education forum focused on new innovations	
One minute preceptorship (Gallagher, et al. 2012)	Using a weekly Team briefing for explaining weekly priorities.
Simulation of a cancer MDT (Winter, et al. 2018)	Watching recorded webinar

According to Blaschke, the balance of vocational learning now accelerates away from andragogical environments and dependence upon others, propelled primarily by the influence of Web technologies (Blaschke 2012). Emancipation of professional education through heutatogy necessitates enlightened organizations to provide learners with the capacity and capability to self-manage their professional development. Connected autonomy in learning may be efficiently assured through the intelligent design of team structures and individual working roles. Acknowledging the cardinality of the day job experiences to professional development demands orientation of working roles and routines to accentuate learning interactions, with a genuine prospect of success manifest through improved patient outcomes.

The challenges of implementation

Surprisingly, training specialists remain disproportionately concerned with formal courses and off-the-job routes to learning across many professions, with less attention devoted to orientating culture and workflow re-engineering. In contrast, a focus on proximal learning, culture and professional development of the clinical team may significantly improve patient outcomes within the NHS.

The management of mortality and morbidity meetings (Sinitsky, et al. 2019) provides a fascinating but ultimately troubled adaptation of clinical routines to prioritize learning; in this case, doctors from across specialisms can review potential medical errors or near misses. Reported conclusions from this activity evidenced a frequent reversion to blaming responses from Team members rather than the intended 'learning and reflection that will change future behaviours'. The failure to establish a safe and trusted environment for Team reflection provides an essential insight into the need for a careful specification of AL initiatives and, specifically, the nurture of a common purpose.

A generalization of preceptorship or, less formally, a simple recognition of the learner practitioner status held by all knowledge workers supports embedding an active learning culture. By empowering individuals to oscillate between tutor and learner, behaviours and habits may be established for ongoing professional development. Preceptorship enables traditional apprenticeship style inquiry but improves the model by avoiding a permanent training hierarchy.

The effective exploitation of active clinical learning opportunities is a problematic expectation from health trained and patient-focused team members and instead requires input from Learning & Development specialists toward an organization-wide dissemination of best-practice and explicit facilitation.

> **PRECEPTORSHIP**
>
> 'A supported period to guide and support learning practitioners in transition to the next stage of their career'.

Neither new nor novel, AL traces back to the thinking and discourse of Jean-Jacques Rousseau (1712–1778). However, current opportunities for collaborative AL have emerged in conjunction with education technology, personal mobile devices, ubiquitous connectivity and asynchronous tools for team collaboration.

Implementation of active learning

An early example of digitally facilitated AL founded upon the video capture of a patient's story through mobile phone was 'Lessons from Chrissy'. The initiative showcased a simplistic use of technology to propagate learning without a high administrative overhead. Chrissy, a patient with a terminal diagnosis, reflected upon her clinical journey as part of a scheduled consultation; in establishing explicit consent to capture and use the footage for service improvement, an authentic and powerful learning resource was developed from within the flow of work. The footage became a critical stimulus to multi-disciplinary learning activities (Winter & Leney 2013).

The shared NHS mission renders AL suited for use across the organization and many multi-disciplinary teams. Moreover, the potential of clinical teams to generate and embed learning is high, arising through the proximal and complementary activities of well qualified and often experienced specialists, each 'working together for patients'. Flexner and Osler asserted the aptness of AL to the clinical context (Tauber 1992). This viewpoint gains further relevance with technological progress and, in recent times, the disruption of professional learning caused by the pandemic.

Mobilization of learning

Efficient mobilization of knowledge is an achievable outcome of embedded AL and manifests alongside democratic processes and widened access to professional development. The SWAG – Velindre Regional Immunotherapy Education Forum (IOEF) exemplifies how such benefits can be strategized and delivered. The IOEF is a multi-disciplinary inclusive oncology group comprising members from a breadth of health care team workers. A single team focus is engaged in agile needs-based learning predicated upon the identified development demands of the membership. The group has no clinical brief but instead agrees on learning priorities and schedules monthly online activities to meet the identified needs. Operating exclusively within core working hours, the group provides a blueprint for agile training and the mobilization of internal expertise.

The Action-Based Curriculum for Immunotherapy project (ABC-4IO), running in the South West region, represents an ambitious use of AL to scale the learning of a clinical team (Winter, et al. 2020). ABC-4IO established a collaboration of the Cancer Centre with a private sector learning consultancy leading to the combined use of best-in-class education technology, microlearning methodology, and specialist medical leadership. The impetus for this partnership is traceable to the revelation of a vocational skills gap evident from staff self-assessed judgements of their Immunotherapy skills and knowledge.

Through positioning AL within working routines, team members are encouraged to understand the process of professional development as continuous and integral. Effective deployment of AL will promote cultural behaviours obligatory for Team excellence and foster a collaborative learning culture compared to a purely cognitive or academic approach. This characterization is consistent with knowledge working and the regulation of personalized medicine. Improved equity of access is a strength of technology-facilitated AL and offsets practical and institutional bias perpetuated in traditional off-the-job training modes. Groups reasonably expected to benefit from enhanced learning from workflow include team members with familial caring duties and others with disabilities hindering access to off-the-job training.

Precision medicine and knowledge work are impossible to deliver through traditional stop-go paradigms of learning. Instead, the workplace must align to the rapidly evolving role of clinicians in the era of personalized medicine. Learning by necessity must become agile, ubiquitous and a cultural expectation. This effort will be unsustainable through the sacrifice of holistic wellbeing and needs delivery within existing duties.

AL in the workflow is powerful due to establishing the cultural status of continuous learning and improvement. Further, AL guarantees an immediate and verifiable relationship between the organizational mission and the pursuit of new skills and knowledge. Achieving balance in new models of clinical training, for example, medical apprenticeships, associate physician schemes and allied health professionals will be imperative to the effective mobilization of the workforce as indicated by HEE England – mobilization framework (England 2021). Identifying barriers to more intensive use of AL requires further investigation but, in probability, reflects enduring anachronism in training strategy, clinician workload and cultural constraints to multi-disciplinary and democratic Team learning.

References

Blaschke, L. M. (2012). Heutagogy and lifelong learning: A review of heutagogical practice and self-determined learning. *International Review of Research in Open and Distance Learning* 13: 56–71.

Cranston, D. (2017). William Osler and his Legacy to Medicine.

England, H. E. (2021). A strategic framework for NHS Knowledge and Library Services in England 2021–2026.

Gallagher, P., Tweed, M., Hanna, S., Winter, H., Hoare, K. (2012). Developing the one-minute preceptor. *Clin Teacher* 9(6): 358–62.

Lombardo, M. M. E., Eichinger, R. W. (1996). *The Career Architect Development Planner* (1st ed.). Minneapolis: Lominger.

Nimmesgern, E., Benediktsson, I., Norstedt, I. (2017). Personalized medicine in Europe. *Clinical and Translational Science* 10(2): 61–63.

Sackett, D. L., Rosenberg, W., Gray, J., Haynes, B., Richardson, S. (1996). Evidence based medicine: What it is and what it isn't. *BMJ* (Clinical research ed.) 312(7023): 71–72.

Sinitsky, D., Gowda, S., Dawas, K., Fernando, B. (2019). Morbidity and mortality meetings to improve patient safety: A survey of 109 consultant surgeons in London, United Kingdom. *Patient Safety in Surgery* 13 (27).

Tauber, A. I. (1992). The two faces of medical education: Flexner and Osler revisited. *Journal of the Royal Society of Medicine* 85(10): 598–602.

Vicente, A. M., Wolfgang Ballensiefen, W., Jönsson, J. (2020). How personalised medicine will transform healthcare by 2030: The ICPerMed vision. *Journal of Translational Medicine* 18(1): 180.

Winter, H. S., Ball, J., Shaw, G., Leney, N., Herbert, C (2020). Micro-learning: A new approach to upskilling and professional development on the management of patients on immunotherapy. *Journal of Clinical Oncology* 38(15_suppl): 11036.

Winter H, Greenhalgh T, Warner N, Segaran A, Handa A. (2018). The teaching of multi-disciplinary cancer care: A flipped classroom approach. *Journal Clinical Oncology* 36_suppl: 11002.

Winter, H. S., Leney, N (2013). Developing an e-learning tool to teach professionalism – "Learning from Chrissy". University of Otago Spotlight on Teaching and Learning Colloquium, New Zealand.

8 A contemplation on four active learning tasks
What do pedagogic theories suggest about them?

Paolo Oprandi

I am often surprised that many weeks of a University module may pass before the students are asked to produce anything, but by the end of the module it is hoped that the students have processed and understood each week's topic. In modules like these, the learning is assumed to be cognitive, solely in the head; the students have read, contemplated over and digested the material, but have not been asked to produce any physical evidence of their learning. In contrast, in modules that take an "active learning" approach to curriculum design, the students regularly produce artefacts which evidence their learning. As a result, an active learning module does not only change what the students know, it changes what the students can produce from what they know. In this article, we explore the theories around four active learning tasks and why through engaging in these tasks students are more likely to feel like experts in the topic and have a long-lasting attachment to it.

Introduction

The theory of active learning has origins that can be found as far back as John Dewey (1986) who made the argument that in order for students to learn one would do better to ask them to do something than directly learn something. One problem with asking students to learn something is that the goal of their learning is at worst *abstract*, because the students do not understand the value of their learning, or at best considered *potential*, because all the student has achieved by learning is to increase their potential to use the knowledge in an authentic situation. In both cases, the goal of learning is less motivational than the goal of producing something or getting something done. That is why when a teacher applies active learning principles to their teaching, they ask students to do something and produce an output. In this article I examine the academic theory behind four active learning

DOI: 10.4324/9781003360032-9

tasks (group podcast, personal written reflection, student generated multiple-choice questions and concept maps) in which the students are asked to produce something, their outputs and the benefits and short fallings, if any, of applying the task to a module curriculum.

It is important to state at this point that I take my analysis from a sociocultural perspective of learning. That is that student learning:

- Is situated in a space, and does not transfer to new spaces without work on the part of the student (Lave and Wenger, 1991).
- Happens between people: the individual, peers and the teacher (Dewey, 1986; Lave and Wenger, 1991; Vygotsky, 1978).
- Is, in most cases, a process of enculturation and adoption of cultural and historical practices: in the cohort, in the department, in the institution, in the discipline and in education more widely (Engeström, 2001).
- Is influenced by the history and agency of the individual (Sannino, Engeström and Lemos, 2016).
- Is influenced by the physical space and objects relating to the students' learning environment (Latour, 2005).

Significantly it is a perspective that understands learning to be a process of becoming someone new. It is a perspective that differs significantly from one that understands learning to be a process of simply acquiring new knowledge in a vacuum of the individual or their environment.

Group podcast

Group podcasts are audio recordings created by groups of students either through talking with each other or recording interviews with people and putting the recording together as a cohesive audio article. The content of the podcast that the students produce will usually include primary or secondary research.

In higher education, formative and summative assessment tasks to produce podcasts is increasing and so is the educational research exploring its effectiveness (Illan, 2019; Phillips, 2017; Snowball and McKenna, 2017). Podcast assessments lessen the reliance on text-based formats for students to evidence their understanding of the topic and hence have been found to provide tutors with flexibility in their approach to teaching (Illan, 2019). Research by Armstrong et al. (2009) indicates that the production of a podcast has increased student engagement with the subject matter, encouraging them to problem solve and to reflect on their own learning. It has been postulated that they foster deep learning in students and improve student retention of knowledge through student engagement in a structured task. Others have suggested that podcasts require students to become knowledge creators because podcast content is generally linked to a real context and the output is usually achieved through collaboration and social negotiation (Pegrum, Bartle and Longnecker, 2015).

In podcasts created in groups, working together comes more naturally than when collaboratively producing text documents. Rajpal and Devi (2011) research suggests that podcasts help students develop their speech, pronunciation, speed and vocabulary by actively using their voice. Ferrer, Lorenzetti and Shaw (2020) found that they develop interpersonal skills such as teamwork and group planning. They argue that podcasts foster positive attitudes towards the materials and describe them as experiential learning tools that improve the students' analytic, communication, cooperation, creativity and technology skills.

In summary, pedagogic theory largely supports the production of podcasts as a strongly formative task and as a summative task that can be used to evidence student understanding. Group podcasts where the production is a social experience involving teamwork and topic-based communication have been found to be even more effective in deepening student engagement.

Personal written reflection

Research has shown time and time again the benefits of reflective writing to learning. The task has been described as active learning because it requires continuous student outputs. As early as the 1900s, Dewey (1933) was interested in reflection as a specialised form of knowledge development in a topic. He described it as:

> a kind of thinking that consists in turning a subject over in the mind and giving it serious thought
>
> (p.3)

His definition of reflection is that it is an:

> "Active, persistent and careful consideration of any belief or supposed form of knowledge" and that, "it includes a conscious and voluntary effort to establish belief upon a firm basis of evidence and rationality."
>
> (p.118)

Kolb (1984) wrote a seminal piece on reflection in the context of experiential learning, which used reflection as a key stage of a four-part learning cycle. In the first stage, the students had concrete experiences that they reflected upon in the second stage. In the third stage, the students transformed their reflections to build upon their abstract conceptualisations and in the final stage they applied these concepts to other situations. The cycle evolves into a spiral of ongoing development from experience, reflection, learning and on to a new experience. Reflection can be thought of as the process of learning from experience or the deepening of learning from an experience through mental processing (Moon, 1999).

Reflection has also been understood in terms of self-assessment and in a meta-analysis of 166 studies, Sitzmann et al. (2010) found that it can shape one's self-efficacy, cognitive learning outcomes and motivation. Reflection helps students identify their academic strengths and weaknesses and this can help them prioritise their efforts. It has been argued that through reflection students can be made more aware of their abilities and shortcomings and this can help them succeed in learning more (Boud, 1995; Yan and Brown, 2017; Yan, Chui and Kp, 2020). Threlfall (2014) reports finding that through active journaling students,

> made remarkably quick progress in becoming critical in their reflections.
>
> (p.317)

In summary, reflective tasks can benefit student learning through deeper interrogation on learning and consolidating new learning with previous experiences. It is a consolidation process of learning through activity. It can lead to more than just the specified learning objectives, and as Moon (2001 p. 15) says, take the student,

> beyond the curriculum, beyond learning defined by learning outcomes, and beyond those of the teacher who is managing the learning
>
> (p.15)

Student generated multiple-choice questions

Many modules use the multiple choice question (MCQ) format to formatively or summatively assess their students, particularly in science, technology, engineering, maths (STEM) and medicine subjects. Due to larger cohorts and increased reliability of computer applications to support the creation and use of MCQs their use is increasing (Nicol, 2007; Snow et al., 2018). Despite some research suggesting that the question format can encourage rote learning, fact memorisation and guessing (McCoubrie, 2004) other literature suggests that they can foster critical thinking and deeper learning when implemented effectively, such as when students take part in the construction of MCQs (Draper, 2009; Nicol, 2007).

Student generation of multiple-choice questions is firmly in the ballpark of an active learning curriculum. There have been a number of studies on the effectiveness of students generating multiple-choice questions for one another in order to improve learning (Draper, 2009; Nicol, 2007; Denny, Luxton-Reilly and Hamer, 2008; Botelho et al., 2018; Posner et al., 2020). The studies have found several perceived benefits to the practice. First, the students need to have a thorough understanding to generate the questions, second the students' needs to know of common misconceptions and finally they will learn to appreciate the depth of understanding required for the module in order to generate appropriate level questions (Botelho et al., 2018). Added benefits have been cited about the use of the multiple-choice questions by students, such as encouraging students to critically engage in how well the MCQ item reflects the learning objectives of the question.

Research by Denny, Luxton-Reilly and Hamer (2008) led them to conclude that the approach promotes a deeper learning experience, increases student motivation and ownership of the material. It provides an impetus for the students to take a closer look at the module learning objectives and the depth of understanding required. There is also increasing research to show that, although MCQs are primarily used in STEM subjects, the student creation of MCQs can benefit students in all disciplines (Botelho et al., 2018).

In summary, student generated multiple choice questions is an active and collaborative activity which can motivate learning. It forms new relationships in the classroom, disrupts the power relations in terms of roles and can motivate students to engage deeper into their studies. The activity can encourage students to familiarise themselves with the learning objectives and level of understanding of the module.

Concept maps

The final active learning task that this article considers are concept maps. These tasks require students to map their understanding of the concepts presented in the module content and link them to personal experiences, previous learning and future ideas. The students connect ideas and word phrases to another and link back to the original idea, word or phrase which prompts learners to make connections between new and old concepts (Sadler, Stevens and Willingham, 2015). They are usually used towards the start of a module when new concepts are being introduced and are used in the development of a deeper expression of the students' understanding. Kaddoura and Yan describe the use of concept maps as,

> an active strategy for teaching students the skills to think critically.
> (2016 p.350)

Islim (2018) says,

> they are forced to link former and current concepts in a meaningful way
> (p.132)

He argues that they provoke students "to think out of the box" and as a result "brings out novel ideas". Lee et al. (2013) have provided evidence that they helps students to visualise their thinking and to organise and summarise knowledge. Karpicke's (2012) studies have indicated that the process of mapping connections facilitates the use of higher order thinking skills (Bloom, 1956). Research from Buldu and Buldu (2010) found that concept maps improve students' awareness of knowledge gaps and misconceptions and help them to understand their own learning process. Zandvakili et al.'s (2019) research focused on multiple connections between different concepts. They found that concept maps deepened student understanding and made them more critical about the topic.

In summary, concept maps are good active learning tools for building ideas and deepening students' understanding of the topic concepts. Usually, they will be the basis of a formative or summative student assessment rather than the final output.

Discussion

Despite having given positive reviews of these tasks, I agree with Bernstein (2018) when he says that active learning tasks are too varied to be able to say whether they are effective per se. From my sociocultural perspective of learning, the four tasks I have listed all help develop what Biesta calls the students' subjectification and increases the emancipatory potential of education (Biesta, 2013).

In almost all cases, active learning tasks increase student engagement (Rifkin et al., 2010), however, that is not to say that the active learning task will improve the summative assessment grades if there has been little change in exam or assessment method. I concur with Rifkin et al. (2010) who say,

> The absence of a rise in exam performance [...] may not reflect the impact on learning. It may be more an indictment of exams as a measure of [...] recall and surface understanding.
>
> (p.48)

As John Dewey (1904) says that students' ability to act on their own intellectual initiative is more of an

> important factor in judging them than their following any particular set method or scheme
>
> (p.27)

such as those used in conformative assessments.

References

Armstrong, G., Tucker, J., & Massad, V. (2009). Interviewing the experts: Student produced podcast. *Journal of Information Technology Education: Innovations in Practice, 8(1)*, 79–90.

Buldu, M., & Buldu, N. (2010). Concept mapping as a formative assessment in college classrooms: Measuring usefulness and student satisfaction. *Procedia: Social and Behavioral Sciences 2(2)*, 2099–104.

Bernstein, D. A. (2018). Does active learning work? A good question, but not the right one. *Scholarship of Teaching and Learning in Psychology, 4(4)*, 290–307.

Biesta, G. (2013). Responsive or responsible? Democratic education for the global networked society. *Policy Futures in Education, 11(6)*, 733–744.

Bloom, B. (1956). *A Taxonomy of Cognitive Objectives.* New York: McKay

Botelho, M. G., Lam, O. L. T., Watt, R. M., Leung, D. Y. P., & Kember, D. (2018). Evaluation of peer-generated MCQs to assess and support learning in a problem-based learning programme. *European Journal of Dental Education, 22(3)*, e358–e363.

Boud, D. (1995). Assessment and learning: Contradictory or complementary. *Assessment for Learning in Higher Education*, pp. 35–48.

Denny, P., Luxton-Reilly, A., & Hamer, J. (2008). *The PeerWise System of Student Contributed Assessment Questions.* Tenth Australasian Computing Education Conference; January; Wollongong, Australia: Conferences in Research and Practice in Information Technology, pp. 69–74.

Dewey, J. (1904). *The Relation of Theory to Practice in Education*. Accessed on 16 July 2021.
Dewey, J. (1933). *How We Think: A Restatement of the Relation of Reflective Thinking to the Educative Process*. Boston, MA: D.C. Heath & Co Publishers.
Dewey, J. (1986). Experience and education. *The Educational Forum, 50(3)*, 241–252.
Draper, S. W. (2009). Catalytic assessment: Understanding how MCQs and EVS can foster deep learning. *British Journal of Educational Technology, 40(2)*, 285–293. DOI: 10.1111/j.1467-8535.2008.00920.x
Engeström, Y. (2001). Expansive learning at work: Toward an activity theoretical reconceptualization. *Journal of education and work, 14*(1), 133–156.
Ferrer, I., Lorenzett, L., & Shaw, J. (2020). Podcasting for social justice: Exploring the potential of experiential and transformative teaching and learning through social work podcasts. *Social Work Education, 39(7)*, 849–865. DOI: 10.1080/02615479.2019.1680619
Illan rua Wall (2019). Podcast as assessment: Entanglement and affect in the law school. *The Law Teacher, 53(3)*, 309–320. DOI: 10.1080/03069400.2018.1554528
Islim, O. F. (2018). Technology-supported collaborative concept maps in classrooms. *Active Learning in Higher Education, 19(2)*, 131–143. DOI: 10.1177/1469787417723231
Kaddoura, V. D., & Yang, Q. (2016). Impact of a concept map teaching approach on nursing students' critical thinking skills. *Nursing & Health Sciences, 18*, 350–354. DOI: 10.1111/nhs.12277
Karpicke, J. D. (2012). Retrieval-based learning: Active retrieval promotes meaningful learning. *Current Directions in Psychological Science, 21(3)*, 157–163.
Kolb, D. A. (1984). *Experiential Learning: Experience as the Source of Learning and Development*. New Jersey: Englewood Cliffs, Prentice-Hall.
Latour, B. (2005). *Reassembling the Social: An Introduction to Actor-Network-Theory*. Oxford: Oxford UP.
Lave, J., & Wenger, E. (1991). *Situated Learning: Legitimate Peripheral Participation*. Cambridge: Cambridge University Press.
Lee, W., Chiang, C. H., Liao, I. C., Lee, M. L., Chen, S. L., & Liang, T. (2013). The longitudinal effect of concept map teaching on critical thinking of nursing students. *Nurse Education Today 33*, 1219–1223.
McCoubrie, P. (2004). Improving the fairness of multiple-choice questions: A literature review. *Medical Teacher, 26(8)*, 709–712. DOI: 10.1080/01421590400013495
Moon, J. (1999). *Learning Journals: A Handbook for Academics, Students and Professional Development*. London: Kogan Page.
Moon, J. (2001). PDP working paper 4: Reflection in higher education learning. *Higher Education Academy*, 1–25.
Nicol, D. (2007). E-assessment by design: Using multiple-choice tests to good effect. *Journal of Further and Higher Education, 31(1)*, 53–64. DOI: 10.1080/03098770601167922

Pegrum, M., Bartle, E., & Longnecker, N. (2015). Can creative podcasting promote deep learning? The use of podcasting for learning content in an undergraduate science unit. *British Journal of Educational Technology, 46(1),* 142–152. DOI: 10.1111/bjet.12133

Phillips, B. (2017). Student-produced podcasts in language learning–exploring student perceptions of podcast activitie. *IAFOR Journal of Education, 5(3),* 157–171.

Posner, L. P., Schoenfeld-Tacher, R., Hedgpeth, M. W., & Royal, K. (2020). Exploring the effects of authoring and answering peer-generated multiple-choice questions. *Education in the Health Professions, 3(1),* 16.

Rajpal, S., & Devi, V. A. (2011). Podcast: Enhancing listening and speaking skills. *Language in India, 11(10),* 259–269.

Rifkin, W. D., Longnecker, N., Leach, J., Davis, L., & Orthia, L. (2010). Students publishing in new media: Eight hypotheses–a house of cards?. *International Journal of innovation in Science and mathematics Education, 18(1),* 43–54.

Sadler, K. C., Stevens, S., & Willingham, J. C. (2015). Collaborative Concept Maps. *Science Scope, 38(9),* 38.

Sannino, A., Engeström, Y., & Lemos, M. (2016). Formative interventions for expansive learning and transformative agency. *Journal of the Learning Sciences, 25(4),* 599–633.

Sitzmann, T., Ely, K., Brown, K. G., & Bauer, K. N. (2010). Self-assessment of knowledge: A cognitive learning or affective measure?. *Academy of Management Learning & Education, 9*(2), 169–191.

Snow, S., Wilde, A., Denny, P., & Schraefel, M. C. (2019). A discursive question: Supporting student-authored multiple choice questions through peer-learning software in non-STEMM disciplines. *British Journal of Educational Technology, 50(4),* 1815–1830.

Snowball, J. D., & McKenna, S. (2017). Student-generated content: An approach to harnessing the power of diversity in higher education, *Teaching in Higher Education, 22(5),* 604–618. DOI: 10.1080/13562517.2016.1273205

Threlfall, S. J. (2014) E-journals: towards critical and independent reflective practice for students in higher education. *Reflective practice, 15(3),* 317–332.

Vygotsky, L. S. (1978). Socio-cultural theory. *Mind in Society, 6,* 52–58.

Yan, Z., & Brown, G. T. (2017). A cyclical self-assessment process: Towards a model of how students engage in self-assessment. *Assessment & Evaluation in Higher Education, 42(8),* 1247–1262.

Yan, Z., Chiu, M. M., & Ko, P. Y. (2020). Effects of self-assessment diaries on academic achievement, self-regulation, and motivation. *Assessment in Education: Principles, Policy & Practice, 27(5),* 562–583.

Zandvakili, E., Washington, E., Gordon, E. W., Wells, C., & Mangaliso, M. (2019). *Teaching Patterns of Critical Thinking: The 3CA Model—Concept Maps, Critical Thinking, Collaboration, and Assessment.* London: SAGE Open. DOI: 10.1177/2158244019885142

Conclusion
Isobel Gowers

Although the chapters in this Focus examine the theory of active learning through very different lenses, as you might expect there are several common themes that re-occur throughout. Student agency; playfulness; scaffolding of active learning tasks; learning places and appropriate assessment tasks are a few of the standout ones.

Student agency

Whether we talk about students as partners, student agency, student engagement or student choice, from the theories explored in this Focus there seems to be little doubt that at the heart of an active learning approach is the idea of being student centred. In her chapter, Mary Jacob referred to the writing of Chickering and Gamson (1987), who refer to 'talk, write and make', and Bonwell and Eison (1991), who discuss 'doing', to draw the conclusion that during active learning students are carrying out tasks through which they learn.

In his chapter, Paolo Oprandi also talks about the increased motivation of producing something or getting something done, compared to learning something as the sole goal of an activity. Bringing these together, I would take it further than that and hypothesise that active learning is about students creating their own learning, through talking, writing, making and doing amongst other things. To be able to do this learning and teaching must be student centred and must allow students agency to make decisions about and the room to create their own learning.

This is validated in Roy Hanney's chapter where he specifically talked about the idea of agency referring to both audience and learner agency. Through empowering of students and giving them some control over their learning we can provide additional motivation for students to learn. Using active learning pedagogies, such as using playful

DOI: 10.4324/9781003360032-10

techniques as suggested by Roy Hanney, leaves the gaps that are open for the students to explore as they choose.

Taking another twist on student agency, Christina Magkoufopoulou discusses the links between transformational learning and active learning. Being giving the space to not only assimilate and apply new knowledge but also to reframe existing knowledge can empower students. It is not just about the knowledge they are gaining now but also about using the knowledge they already have by looking at it in a different way.

As a final note on this Nick Leney and Helen Winter refer to both the importance of two-way communication in active learning and the need for an egalitarian approach where both student and teacher are equals. This allows students agency and enables students to become partners in their own learning journey.

Playfulness

Roy Hanney, Tab Betts and Sarah Honeychurch all emphasise the importance of playfulness in learning. The ability to go beyond just discussing something made me think about curiosity. As children we will often take things apart to try and understand them better. We then try and put them back together, which is when the problems sometimes occur but whether we are successful or not this is an invaluable learning experience. The idea of going further than just reporting on something but instead trying to fathom out how it works and then making our own is an aspect of play that would be useful in many education contexts.

Scaffolding active learning tasks

How important is it that the students understand what is happening and how active learning might be different from what they expected learning to be like at university? Mary Jacob talks about starting active learning early to help students to develop appropriate expectations. Students often come to university with pre-conceived ideas of how teaching will happen. This is not helped by the portrayal of university teaching on television. Many students come expecting to be lectured at. So, to start with we might need to do work so that students know what to expect learning and teaching to be about at university but it goes beyond that. Students need to know that during active learning it is a safe space to think outside the box, to take risks and that they have permission to experiment. This is crucial to allow students to fully participate in active learning, particularly in the types of activity that Roy Hanney talks about using play and playfulness for creative problems solving and developing ideation skills.

Where does active learning happen?

Active learning is naturally synonymous with a move away from delivery in large tiered lecture theatres. As Sam Elkington highlights in his chapter learning no longer occurs only in classrooms, although one might argue that it never did only occur in the classroom, but the point Sam Elkington is making is that digital has provided new opportunities for places to learn. In addition, digitally facilitated active learning is highlighted by Nick Leney and Helen Winter where they discuss the use of Chrissy's story as a critical stimulus in multi-disciplinary learning activities.

There has been considerable research and scholarly output focusing on learning spaces, often looking at informal learning spaces on campus as well as digital learning environments. During the Covid-19 pandemic hybrid teaching became a necessity but there are some arguments for continuing to offer a mix of face-to-face and online synchronous delivery that allows student choice and greater flexibility. The chapters within this Focus touch on the importance of giving consideration to the digital learning space, it is important that we ensure both our face to face and digital learning spaces embrace the principles and ethos of active learning and that the digital space does not just become a repository of artefacts but instead is used to support a collaborative, engaging learning environment.

With a growing interest in authentic learning, again there is the potential to move away from traditional learning spaces and moving into more employment or employment simulated environments with or without the help of technology. Nick Leney and Helen Winter highlight the importance of on-the-job learning that will occur both in vocational courses, such as degree apprenticeships, but is also commonplace in further study completed by graduates once they are employed. It is important that as well as appropriate active learning tasks being used in professional learning settings that students are prepared, during higher education for learning on the job. These additional learning environments can bring new challenges for staff and students as well as providing great opportunities for active learning.

Appropriate assessment tasks

Paolo Oprandi highlights something that I have found within my own practice too, although we are seeing more inclusion of active learning tasks within the curriculum this still has not filtered through to assessments. This is surprising when taking an active learning and assessment approach, as suggested by Sarah Honeychurch, can help deal with educational issues such as the stress of assessment for learners, marking workload for staff and lack of engagement by students with formative work. There needs to be more use of some of the theory highlighted in this Focus to support the educational change leading to more appropriate assessment tasks that will benefit both students and staff.

Moving towards an active learning philosophy

This special moves from the theoretical and frameworks, to developing new frameworks to how we can start to apply theory and frameworks to practice. Throughout we have seen some common themes develop but overall taking a holistic approach that is student centred has come out as the strongest principle. Although there has been a trend to move towards active learning adopting this principle, it is yet to be embraced as an all-encompassing philosophy by many. The theoretical aspects of active learning and how we approach it, as evidenced in this Focus, can help inform how we can further expand its adoption.

References

Bonwell, C. C. and Eison, J. A. (1991) *Active learning: Creating excitement in the classroom.* Washington, DC: School of Education and Human Development, George Washington University.

Chickering, A. W. and Gamson, Z. F. (1987) Seven principles for good practice in undergraduate education. *AAHE Bulletin*, pp. 3–7.

Index

Note: **Bold** page numbers refer to tables; *italic* page numbers refer to figures and page numbers followed by "n" denote endnotes.

ABC learning design (ABC LD) 49–50; mapping with online engagement 54, **54**
academic research process 7, 8, 22
acquisition 49, 50, 53
Action-Based Curriculum for Immunotherapy project (ABC-4IO) 70
active category, ICAP model 51
Active Cognitive Task (ACT) 47–50, 55; task component of 51
active learning (AL) 1, 3, 7–8, 67, 84; definitions of 46–48; educational issues 27; in higher education 16; implementation of 69–70; literature on 2; need for 67–68, **68**; *vs.* passive learning 67, **68**; philosophy 85; practice 66–67; promotion of 46; role within transformative learning experiences 35; scaffolding tasks 83–84; serendipity of 30; theoretical approaches to 2; two-way communication of 67; *see also* learning
active learning groups, learners into 30–31
active learning online: challenges of 48; in classroom 48; and taxonomy 51
active learning strategy 37; effectiveness of 1; playfulness as 20
"active learning university" 2

affinity spaces 31
affordances 57, 59, 60
agency 20–21
Anderson, L. W. 50
Aristotle: *mythos* 13; *Poetics* 7
Armstrong, G. 74
assessment tasks 85
autonomy: in learning 68; of play 20–21

behavioural engagement 52, 54
Bennett, S. 28
Bernstein, D. A. 2, 78
Betts, Tab 2, 83
Biesta, G. 78
Blaschke, L. M. 68
Bloom's taxonomy 11; of educational objectives *50*, 50–51
Bonwell, C. C. 47, 51, 82
Boyd, B. 21, 22
bricolage 2, 27, 29; derivation of 29; holistic active learning using 32; implicit in 29–30; learners 31; practice of 29
Buldu, M. 78
Buldu, N. 78

Campbell, Joseph 7, 13, 14
character arcs, of teachers and learners 12–13
Cheng, S. H. 2
Chickering, A. W. 46–47, 82

Chi's framework 51–52
Chiu, P. H. P. 2
classroom-based teaching 49
coactive learning 60; strategies 59–60
cognitive bias 19
cognitive engagement 52, 54
collaboration 49, 53; fostering meaningful 60–61
collaborative engagement 52, 54
collaborative notetaking tools 60
collaborative storytelling 10, 11
collaborative work active learning 59, 60
Collaboratorium 24, 25
communicative discourse 42–43
communicative learning 36
community of practice (CoP) 31, 38–39
concept maps 77–78
constructionism 29, 30
constructive category, ICAP model 51
constructive feedback 30
cooperative learning 59, 60
Covid-19 pandemic 1, 84
creative play time 11–12
creativity 19, 23; and innovation 22; stages of 20
critical reflection 36, 43
critical self-reflection 41
cross-mapping active learning frameworks 52–53, **53**; with online engagement **54**, 54–55

Denny, P. 77
Devi, V. A. 75
Dewey, John 73, 75, 79
digital creators 28
digital learning 57; tools 58, 60, 62, 64
digital learning space 84
discussion 49, 53; encouraging rich interactions and 61–63
discussion-solution process 60

EBM *see* evidence-based medicine (EBM)
education: issues of 27; technology, change and innovation in 58–59; transforming landscape of 34; *see also* higher education (HE)
educators 29, 35, 36, 41, 64; challenge for 60; coactive participation of student and 58; learners and 27
effective teaching 13–14
Eison, J. A. 47, 51, 82
Elkington, Sam 3, 84
Ellis, R. A. 58
emotional engagement 52, 54
employment, transforming landscape of 34
Engeström, Yrjö 35
evidence-based medicine (EBM) 66
experiential learning 76; self-directed structure of 28; theory 37–38
Experimentarium 24, 25
Exploratorium 24, 25

face-to-face teaching 1, 55, 60, 62, 63, 84
feedback 29, 30; constructive 30; formative 31, 32, 64
Ferrer, I. 75
flexible learning environments 57
Flexner, Abraham 70
formative feedback 31, 32, 64
for-the-sake-of-which of play 23, 24
frame of reference 36–38, 40, 43n1
functional fixedness 2, 19, 25

game-based learning 7
games 22–23
gamification 7, 24
Gamson, Z. F. 46–47, 82
Gee, J. P. 31
gender achievement gaps 2
Goodyear, P. 58
The Ground Itself (Pipkin) 8
group podcasts 74–75

Habermas, J. 36
Hamer, J. 77
hanging out 28–29
"Hanging Out, Messing Around, Geeking Out" (HOMAGO) 28
Hanney, Roy 2, 82–84
Hao, Q. 1
Harmon, Dan 7

Index

hero's journey 7, 13–15
higher education (HE) 58; active learning, play and storytelling in 16; landscape 34; learning environment for 1; massification of 34; metric-driven ecology of 22; online engagement framework for 52
holistic active learning 32
Honeychurch, Sarah 83, 85
hybrid learning 57; and challenges to space and pedagogy 57–59; complexity of 64
hybrid teaching 64, 84

ICAP model *see* interactive-constructive-active-passive (ICAP) model
informative active learning 37, 40, *40*, 42
informative learning 37
instructor-focused teaching 58
instrumental learning 36
interactive category, ICAP model 51
interactive-constructive-active-passive (ICAP) model 51–52
interactive experiential story 10–11
International Consortium for Personalized Medicine 66
investigation 49, 53, 54
Islim, O. F. 78
Ito, Mimi 28

Jacob, Mary 2, 82, 83
James, A. 23
jamming sessions 12
Jarvis, Peter 38

Kaddoura, V. D. 78
Karpicke, J. D. 78
Kegan, R. 36
knowledge 7–11, 13; behaviour/quantity of 36; mobilization of 70; theory of 29
knowledge acquisition 23
knowledge construction, play in 22
knowledge working 71
Kolb, D. A. 37, 76; experiential learning theory 37

Laurillard, D. 49
Lave, J. 31, 38
learner agency, of play 20–21
learners: in active learning 27; into active learning groups 30–31; character arcs of 12–13; and educators 27; on hero's journey 13–15
learning: as "active process" 49; autonomy in 68; challenges of implementation 68–69; cognitive dimension of 52; conventional forms of 61; defined as 37–38; functionality of 36; goal of 73; mobilization of 70–71; patterns within NHS clinical teams 67; playfulness in 83; process of 27; sociocultural perspective of 74, 78; theory of 29; through worked examples of scenarios/problem tasks 63–64; transformation plays in 35; *see also* active learning (AL)
Learning and Teaching Enhancement Unit 46, 48
learning community: creative play time 11–12; of staff and students 10; of staff, students and stakeholders 13
learning design 10, 30, 32; storytelling in 10–11
learning environment 1, 36, 40–43, 58, 84; flexible 57
learning jamming sessions 12
learning place 58
'learning through social making' 29
Lee, W. 78
legitimate peripheral participation 39
Leney, Nick 3, 83, 84
Lepper, M. R. 9
live polling/quiz tools 62
Lorenzett, L. 75
Luxton-Reilly, A. 77

Magkoufopoulou, Christina 2, 83
Malone, T. W. 9
McKeachie, W. J. 2
mental activities 21
Mezirow, J. 35–38, 41, 43n1
Michelangelo 20

Microsoft Forms 62
Microsoft OneNote/Padlet 63
mind gym 23–25
mobilization framework 71
model of assessment 32
model of learning 29
models: neo-liberal 25; of storytelling 14
modern learners 28
morbidity meetings, management of 69
multiple-choice question (MCQ), student generated 76–77

neo-liberal model 25
neuroscience 22; of play 20–21
Nørgärd, R.T. 22–24

online engagement framework, for higher education 52; cross-mapping active learning frameworks **54**, 54–55
on-the-job learning 84
Oprandi, Paolo 3, 82, 85
Osler, Sir William 66, 70
ownership 28, 42, 59, 77

Papert, Seymour 29
Passarelli, A. M. 37
passive learning 51; active learning vs. 67, **68**
Patchwork Text 32
pedagogic theory 75
pedagogy: challenges to 57–59; playful 25
Perović, N. 49
personalized medicine (PM) 66, 67, 71
personal written reflection 75–76
person-environment system 59
physical activities 21
play 7–9; challenges 19–20; creative play time 11–12; in higher education 16; in knowledge construction 22; learner agency, autonomy, and neuroscience of 20–21; as pedagogic strategy 21–23
playful learning, principles for 24
playfulness 20, 24, 25, 83

playful pedagogy 25
playful university 23–25
PM *see* personalized medicine (PM)
podcasts 74–75
Poetics (Aristotle) 7
Postgraduate Certificate in Teaching in HE (PGCTHE) 46
practice 49, 53, 54
preceptorship 69
precision medicine 71
Prensky, M. 28
production 49, 53, 54
project-based learning 59, 60

Rajpal, S. 75
Redmond, P. 52, 54
reflection: critical 36, 43; definition of 75; personal written 75–76; seminal piece on 76
Rifkin, W. D. 79
Rousseau, Jean-Jacques 69

science, technology, engineering, maths (STEM) 76, 77
Shaw, J. 75
Sitzmann, T. 76
Smith, S. 22
social constructionism 29
social engagement 52, 54
social learning theory 38–39
socio-cultural structure 27
socio-cultural theory 2
Socrative tool 62
space: affinity 31; challenges to 57–59; digital and physical tools and 58; digital learning 84; traditional lecture theatre learning 1
Staricoff, Marcelo 11
story circle 7, 14
storytelling 7–9; in higher education 16; in learning design 10–11
student agency 82–83
Svinicki, M. D. 2
SWAG – Velindre Regional Immunotherapy Education Forum (IOEF) 70
synthesising frameworks 48–49; ABC learning design 49–50; Bloom's taxonomy of educational objectives

50, 50–51; interactive-constructive-active-passive model 51–52; online engagement framework for higher education 52

teachers: character arcs of 12–13; cognitive engagement 54; complex of distributed learning spaces 64; emotional engagement 54
teaching: classroom-based 49; designing of 30; effective 13–14; face-to-face 1, 55, 60, 62, 63, 84; hybrid 64, 84; instructor-focused 58; session, stages of 14–15
theory of active learning 73, 82
theory of knowledge 29
theory of learning 29
theory-practice nexus 20
Threlfall, S. J. 76
traditional lecture-based dissemination methods 1
traditional lecture theatre learning space 1
traditional teacher-centred pedagogies 7
transformational learning 35, 36, 83
transformations 12, 21, 25, 35
transformative active learning 40, *40*; framework for 41–42
transformative learning: social aspect of 41; theoretical exploration of 35–41, *40*
transformative learning theory 35–37, 41
tutor 14–15

University of Active Learning, Play and Storytelling 7, 9–10

vocational learning, balance of 68
Vygotsky, Lev 38

Wenger, E. 31, 38
Wenger-Trayner, B. 43n4
Wenger-Trayner, E. 43n4
Winter, Helen 3, 83, 84

XCa learning community 13

Yang, Q. 78
Young, C. 49

Zandvakili, E. 78
Zone of Proximal Development 38, 43n3

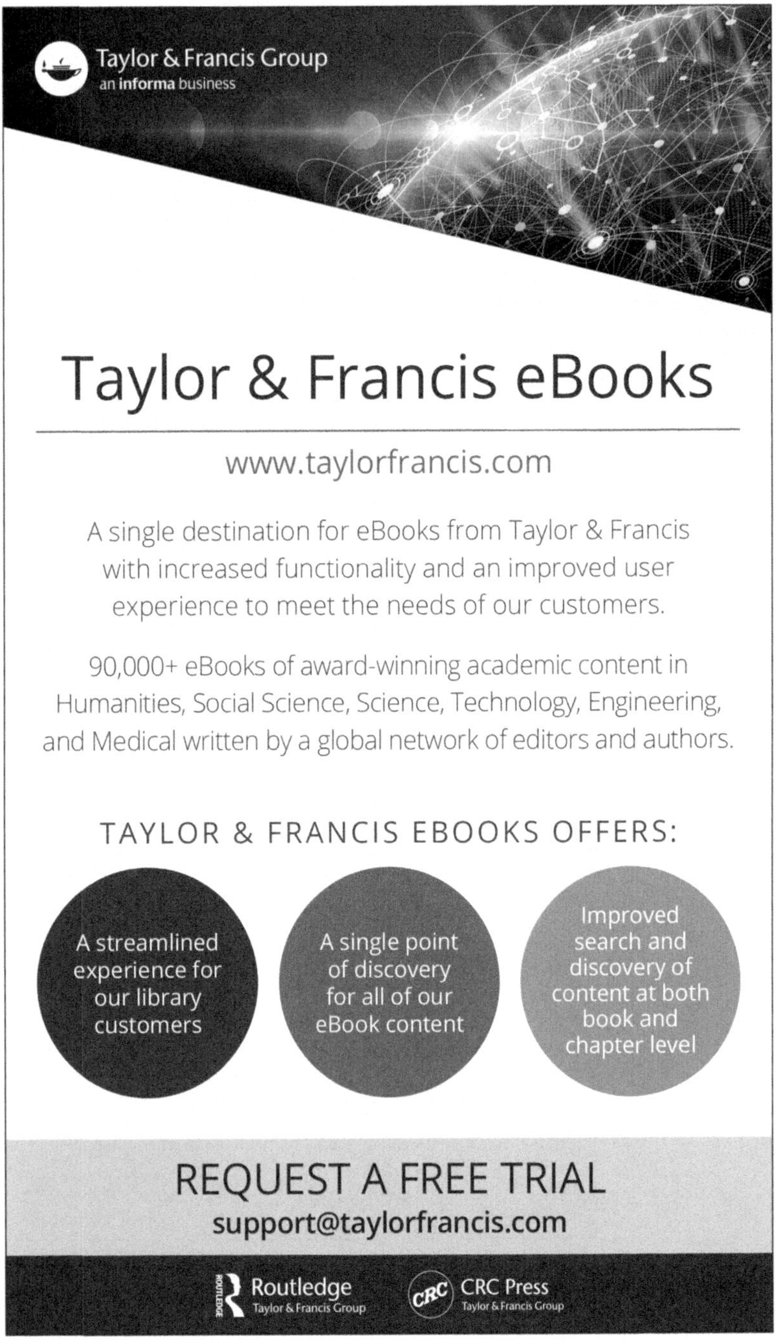
Taylor & Francis Group
an informa business
Taylor & Francis eBooks
www.taylorfrancis.com
A single destination for eBooks from Taylor & Francis with increased functionality and an improved user experience to meet the needs of our customers.
90,000+ eBooks of award-winning academic content in Humanities, Social Science, Science, Technology, Engineering, and Medical written by a global network of editors and authors.
TAYLOR & FRANCIS EBOOKS OFFERS:
A streamlined experience for our library customers
A single point of discovery for all of our eBook content
Improved search and discovery of content at both book and chapter level
REQUEST A FREE TRIAL
support@taylorfrancis.com
Routledge
Taylor & Francis Group
CRC Press
Taylor & Francis Group